SEA LEVEL RISING

The Chatham Story

Bill Sargent

Schiffer Publishing Ltd®

4880 Lower Valley Road   Atglen, Pennsylvania   19310

This book is dedicated to the memory of my mother Jessie Fay Sargent, who fried many a flounder on Monomoy Island, and Laura Broad, who loved her camp "Driftwood" on North Beach.

Copyright © 2009 by Bill Sargent
Library of Congress Control Number: 2008943516

Designed by Bruce Waters
Type set in Zurich BT

ISBN: 978-0-7643-3261-6
Printed in the United States of America

Schiffer Books are available at special discounts for bulk purchases for sales promotions or premiums. Special editions, including personalized covers, corporate imprints, and excerpts can be created in large quantities for special needs. For more information contact the publisher:

Published by Schiffer Publishing Ltd.
4880 Lower Valley Road
Atglen, PA 19310
Phone: (610) 593-1777; Fax: (610) 593-2002
E-mail: Info@schifferbooks.com

For the largest selection of fine reference books on this and related subjects, please visit our web site at **www.schifferbooks.com**
We are always looking for people to write books on new and related subjects. If you have an idea for a book please contact us at the above address.

This book may be purchased from the publisher.
Include $5.00 for shipping.
Please try your bookstore first.
You may write for a free catalog.

In Europe, Schiffer books are distributed by
Bushwood Books
6 Marksbury Ave.
Kew Gardens
Surrey TW9 4JF England
Phone: 44 (0) 20 8392 8585; Fax: 44 (0) 20 8392 9876
E-mail: info@bushwoodbooks.co.uk
Website: www.bushwoodbooks.co.uk

Contents

Acknowledgments & Apologies...5

Foreword: A Swiss Interlude 10

Chapter One: Camp Crowell...16
      The Patriot's Day Storm, April 16, 2007

Chapter Two: The Wager 22
      April 24, 2007

Chapter Three: "Throwing Out the Baby with the Bath Water"...32
      July 31, 2007

Chapter Four: The Shoe Camp Incident.......................................42
      August 9, 2007

Chapter Five: The Attack 52
      August 11, 2007

Chapter Six: "Driftwood" 58
      Labor Day Weekend, 2007

Chapter Seven: The Wreck...64
      September 5, 2007

Chapter Eight: Fieldwork 74
      October 16, 2007

Chapter Nine: Donald Harriss 84
      October 26, 2007

Chapter Ten: Rogues and Patterns, Patterns and Rogues............94
      Hurricane Noel, November 3, 2007

Chapter Eleven: Five Days in November 102
      November, 2007

Chapter Twelve: A Day of Thanksgiving 108
      November 24, 2007

Chapter Thirteen: La Nina 116
      December 7, 2007

Chapter Fourteen: The End of the Year. The End of an Era? 122

    December 28, 2007

Chapter Fifteen: Fred's True Love 128

    January 12, 2008

Chapter Sixteen: Problems and Paradigms 138

    A mid-January course correction

Chapter Seventeen: Backlash and Batty 146

    January 26, 2008

Chapter Eighteen: The Inletcam 154

    January 28, 2008

Chapter Nineteen: Mid-Winter Blues 159

    February 8th, 2008

Chapter Twenty: Diastole; The Heart at Rest 166

    March 11, 2008

Chapter Twenty-One: The Wooden Tent 176

    March 19, 2008

Chapter Twenty-Two: April Fool's Day? 181

    April 1, 2008

Chapter Twenty-Three: Expert Testimony 187

    June 26, 2008

Chapter Twenty-Four: Town Hall Camp; 196

    Fourth of July Weekend

Chapter Twenty- Five: Plover, Seals, and a Spadefoot Toad 201

    July 17, 2008

Chapter Twenty-Six: Playing "Wolf" 210

    September, 2008

Chapter Twenty-Seven: The Future 216

Epilogue 224

Acknowledgments & Apologies

Shortly after finishing the proposal for this book I received a call from Ethan Daniels. Ethan explained he was an underwater photographer who had spent his summers on Pleasant Bay and been influenced by my books. Now he wanted to write an article about all the changes I had seen in Pleasant Bay since writing my first book, *Shallow Waters*. I was aghast at the ageist implications of the request, but heartily agreed.

Of course the biggest change that had taken place in Pleasant Bay was the new inlet that had broken through Nauset Beach only a few short months before. It also turned out that Ethan was doing this project for an arts practicum at Boston University's Center for the Digital Arts. The Center had been started by Ethan's uncle, Bob Daniels, who had also grown up on, and loved, Pleasant Bay. One thing led to another and we all finally agreed to produce a film that would present Pleasant Bay as a case study to investigate the effects of sea level rise.

Several dedicated, though autoless, videographers helped us make the film. When I refer to videographers in this book, I am mostly referring to the intrepid Susan Haney, Caluh Escovar, and Franco Saatchi who were always willing, even eager, to go out in the worst sorts of weather.

Throughout the summer Ethan and I dutifully hauled our equipment out to the outer beach every day by boat. The camp owners were initially bemused at our audacity, but eagerly invited us in. We came to know many of the camp owners as well as our own families. Later, I was with the families when they were facing losing their camps and beloved way of life. We became good friends through sharing some of the most intense experiences of their lives. I particularly want to thank Rob Crowell, Donald Harriss, and Russell Broad for their hospitality and skills driving us down the beach. Rob, even though your motor broke down on the coldest day in October, I continue to admire your considerable boating expertise

At 86, Donald Harriss was easily the youngest acting person on the beach. He was always eager to get up before sunrise and drive a hundred-fifty miles down from the North Shore and through the deserted streets of Boston in order to arrive on Nauset Beach just as the sun was breaking the horizon. The first thing Donald would do, as soon as we hit the beach, was to whip out his cell phone and call all the many members of his far flung family to tell them that we were on the beach and to turn on their computers so they could see us waving back at them from the "Inletcam" stationed on the mainland. Despite his losses Donald treated each expedition down the beach as if it were his first trip to Disneyland.

Ted Keon and Graham Giese were our two main experts on this project. They were particularly helpful at both interpreting the long range behavior of the inlet and cautioning me when I was about to over interpret a short term phenomena. During those times they had to put up with my gentle reminders that they had been the experts who had predicted that the inlet would fill in in a few weeks. Now I can say through experience that an inlet is indeed a fiendishly complex phenomenon to understand.

Half way through this book Donald Harriss introduced me by e-mail to Dan Ryan. Dan was a pathologist who had a house on the mainland opposite the inlet. During the summer he installed a camera that could inspect both the condition of the inlet and his beach. At first it had been just a family novelty, but as the inlet expanded and houses came into jeopardy the camera became a useful scientific tool.

Dan also introduced me to his brother Bill Ryan, a professional meteorologist at Penn State. Bill had access the National Oceanographic and Atmospheric Administration's offshore wave buoys and the National Weather Service's large Cray mainframe computers that produce three slightly different weather models throughout each day. Bill was able to feed us this information along with detailed forecasts of how high the waves would be breaking on Nauset Beach and how close the low pressure systems would track toward Chatham. The "Inletcam," as we came to call it, provided us with precise measurements of how much erosion had occurred. We were able to put all these pieces together and provide forecasts of how much erosion to expect. These erosion forecasts helped people make crucial decisions about when to remove their homes. Up until the end of the first year, the Ryans preferred to stay anonymous. Now their camera has been replaced by a town-owned camera, and I can say that I, and the town of

Chatham, owe a huge debt of gratitude to the entire Ryan family.

As I was finishing this book, Thadd Eldredge and Tim Wood came to the fore. Thadd is a local surveyor who was hired by the camp owners but became as obsessed as I was in figuring out the fascinating ways of the new inlet. Tim Wood is the editor of Chatham's local newspaper who started www.chathamnorthbeach.com, a website that became an invaluable resource and the prime forum for disseminating information about the inlet. Each of us eagerly awaited the others' data, whether it be my daily erosion forecasts, Thadd's GPS surveys, or Ted Keon's aerial photographs. All these new methods of understanding the inlet stood in marked contrast to those used only twenty years before when people had to wait for several months for experts to release large government-sponsored studies that could only tell you what the inlet had been like half a year before.

Finally I would like to add a note on nomenclature. Geographical names are a fluid commodity on Cape Cod. I remember the bewilderment I first felt when someone told me they lived beyond Sargent's point. I had never heard the term before. Since I grew up in Orleans I have always referred to the outer beach as Nauset Beach. But in Chatham, the same beach is called North Beach. It used to be, that nobody could tell you why North Beach was called North Beach. It really wasn't north of anything. It was only after the 1987 inlet opened that suddenly everything became crystal clear. Now Chatham had both a North Beach and a South Beach as it had in the 1800s when the inlet was in the same location and the beaches had been first named. But the term North Beach had persisted well after South Beach had broken apart and retreated into the mainland back in the early 1900s.

After the 2007 inlet opened, however, Chathamites continued the same naming logic, referring to North Beach, North Beach Island, South Beach and Monomoy—though nobody could quite agree on where South Beach ended, and the former Monomoy Island began. If we continue in this vein we will have North Beach, North North Beach Island, South South Beach Island and South South Beach—Monomoy Island. Consequently I have chosen to call the three present entities, Nauset Beach, Lighthouse Island and Monomoy. I don't really expect that anyone will adopt this simpler Orleans-based lexicon, but I have tried to stay true to it throughout this manuscript.

I hope the people of Chatham will forgive my taking such nomenclatural liberties. Other than that, this has been a grand collaboration. Scores of people have helped me with their interest, logistical help, and hospitality. I have tried to mention everyone in this book, and hope I have told your stories well.

Orleans
2008

Foreword
A Swiss Interlude

Shortly before starting to write this book, the Swiss government invited me to join a media tour of European companies battling global warming. It was a little embarrassing for an American to see how far we trail the Continent in developing green technology.

Our first stop was Le Grande Dixence dam, sixty miles east of Geneva. When an American first sees the Alps he might think of schussing the slopes, but when a Swiss national sees the Alps, he sees white energy. Two thirds of the precipitation that falls on Switzerland gets locked up in her so-called eternal glaciers. When the glaciers melt they release all that potential energy into bubbling cascades of life giving, life enhancing water. For centuries the Swiss harnessed these glacial waters to irrigate their pastures, meadows, and vineyards.

After World War II, however, Switzerland realized it could also harness these glacial waters for energy. The Swiss government built over a hundred miles of underground tunnels to direct melt water from thirty-five major glaciers in the Valais Canton, and stored it in a mile-long lake behind a massive gravity dam, 2400 meters above sea level.

Le Grande Dixence dam is probably the least known major engineering structure in the world. It is more massive than the Great Pyramid of Egypt, rises higher than the Eiffel tower of Paris and is longer and built at a higher elevation than the Hoover dam. And, there I was, an American tourist thinking nothing was bigger than the Hoover dam! In fact if you poured all the concrete used to build Le Grande Dixence into a five foot wall, it would encircle our planet at the equator. But a Chinese journalist in our group pointed out that the Three Gorges Dam would be even larger.

"Ah oui, c'est vrai," said our Swiss host. "But, we did not have to displace a single human being. You will displace, what, several hundred million people in many cities and villages, non?"

Le Grande Dixence has remained unknown even to most Swiss tourists, in spite of a charming film that hikers can see only after they descend deep into the dam's living, breathing, concrete heart. In spite of its humble use as a touristy documentary, the film had the distinct feel of a classic. We saw canister after canister of cement being ferried overhead in dizzying aerial shots reminiscent of similar scenes by Leni Riefenstahl, and we saw untold tons of concrete being dumped and compacted into preexisting molds. It was only when the credits rolled that I realized that this was the first film ever made by Jean luc Goddard. As a student the famed French director poured concrete at the dam by day, and labored on his epic all night.

After twenty years of round-the-clock construction, the dam was finally finished in 1961, three years ahead of schedule and under budget. Today Le Grande Dixence helps Switzerland produce 60 percent of all its electrical energy needs through hydroelectric dams. The hydroelectric power is so plentiful that the Swiss government sells it to France during the day when the rates are high, then buys nuclear generated electricity back from French at night when the rates are low. The Swiss then use this cheap French power to pump water back into their dams so they can sell more electricity back to France the next day—at thirty times more than they paid for it!

Switzerland uses all this clean, cheap, hydroelectric energy to run the vast network of electrically powered trains and subways that weave through the country like the inner workings of a finely tuned Swiss watch. Yet despite all this, Switzerland still retains five, almost never mentioned, nuclear power plants that it has voted to discontinue in the near future.

We heard an impressive array of scientists, government officials, and businessmen from France, Germany, Denmark and Norway speaking at an energy conference held in Lucerne. After the 1970s oil crisis, almost all of the European countries embarked on an ambitious program to develop clean, cheap, energy technologies. They designed new more efficient cars, trains, and household appliances and built large new arrays of photovoltaic cells and wind turbines.

We also met with Bertrand Piccard, the scion of a long line of Swiss engineers. His grandfather was the first human to ever ascend into the stratosphere in a balloon he had designed himself. His father was the first human to ever dive to the bottom of the Mariannias Trench, the deepest spot in the world's deepest ocean. Of course it was in a bathysphere he had designed himself. Bertrand showed us his designs for a solar powered aircraft whose wings are so long they could span two football fields. He told us of his project to fly the plane nonstop around the world, powered entirely by solar energy. After finishing his talk he casually drove off in a solar powered car on the first leg of its own round the world expedition. Not a bad transition for the son of a submariner and the grandson of a balloonist.

Although it was heartening to see how much Europeans have done to develop green technology, it was equally disheartening to realize that their thirty years of expensive efforts have not lowered global temperatures one iota. That is the great conundrum with global warming. Even if could stop all carbon emissions tomorrow, there is already so much carbon dioxide in the atmosphere that sea levels and global temperatures will continue to rise throughout most of our lifetimes. This means that no matter what we do, or don't do, about global warming, we still have to deal with its effects.

The point was driven home at the end of yet another long power point presentation on photovoltaic cells. A young businessman dared to mention that only two weeks before, a mountain storm had washed away a village, started a landslide, and caused more than a hundred million dollars in damages. He was making the point that the $350 million dollars that

Switzerland provides to support research and development on photovoltaic cells is a drop in the bucket compared to the problems already being caused by global warming.

But he was also making the more salient point that global warming is not a problem we will face in some hypothetical future. Whether we like it or not, villages like Chatham and cities like New Orleans have become the canaries in the coal mine for the rest of the world. What Chatham is facing today other coastal communities will face tomorrow. We will do well to heed her lessons.

Glacier above Grande Dixieme Dam.

Chapter One
Camp Crowell

The Patriot's Day Storm
April 16, 2007

Robert Crowell fiddled with his battery operated radio one last time before going to bed. The reporters were still bickering about whether the elements were going to interfere with the Boston Marathon. "I'll give you elements," chuckled Rob to himself. So much water was bubbling up through the east wall windowsills that he had to move his bed toward the center of the room. Outside twenty foot waves were towering over the roof line of his thin walled camp. The roar of the southeast gale whistling through the walls made it impossible to hear the radio anyway, so he turned down the kerosene lamp and surrendered to the all encompassing darkness.

Camp Crowell shuddered each time another breaker slammed into the low dunes. They were the only protection the camp had against the full force of the Atlantic. But there was no place on earth Robert Crowell would rather be. Even in an April Nor'easter he enjoyed lying in the dark surrounded by the entrancing power of raw nature.

The old Crowell camp.

Bob knew this tenuous land of sand, sea, and water was an acquired taste. Five generations of Crowells, Nickersons, Eldredges, and Mayos had come out here to live off the land and enjoy seeing the sun rise unimpeded out of the limitlessness expanse of the Atlantic ocean. It wasn't an absolute prerequisite of owning a summer camp that you had to be a direct descendant of one the original families who settled Chatham, but it helped. It helped that one of your ancestors had moved down from the Plymouth Plantation to haggle with the Monomoyick Indians to obtain rights to scythe the marsh hay inside the outer beach. Robert often imagined his relatives sweating in ninety degree heat behind oxen covered in deerflies and greenheads. Later relatives had come out here to hunt ducks in winter and catch bass in summer.

They knew how to rig a broad-beamed fishing boat to sail across Pleasant Bay or tinker with Model T beach buggies so they could drive down the five mile long barrier beach to the two clusters of lonely summer camps. It helped that Bob had seen his father build an outhouse, pump water from a shallow dune well, pile eelgrass against their camp's foundation, and do all the other myriad of chores that made living in a summer camp possible.

As a kid, Bob remembered seeing his father build the first modern summer camp on the outer beach. It had been back in 1960, the year before the Seashore moved in. It had been a lot more casual in those days. A neighbor who wanted to build a summer camp just drove over to Josh Nickerson and asked if he could build a camp on his original Indian deed to the outer beach. It had perplexed the Seashore no end that there were no records or formal plots, just a gentleman's agreement sealed over a late afternoon drink. Now Bob had to pay the Seashore an $8,000 user's fee just to live in his own house.

But it had all been worth it. He remembered staying up for the 3 a.m. high tide so he could see some men jimmy the Old Harbor Life Saving Station onto an ocean going barge and ferry it up to the tip of Provincetown. He remembered when lightning struck their camp in 1970 and when they had to move the camp inland after the 1978 storm and when they had to rebuild their camp on pilings 13 feet above mean high tide after the "no-name storm" in 1991. Bob still liked to use the modest Cape Cod name for the storm rather than "The Perfect Storm" made popular by that young Sebastian Junger kid who surfed up in Truro.

Each repair to the Crowell Camp had given Bob and Maria a few more years to enjoy the beach and allowed another generation of Crowells to get some salt in their blood and sand in their genes. But every year it had also gotten a little harder. Russ and Tim were almost in the twenties now, and Bob wasn't sure how much longer they would want to use the camp. Every year another family would sell their shacks after a divorce, a death, or when they just ran out of family members willing to take on the responsibility. People just didn't have the time anymore. You had to maintain a fleet of boats and beach buggies just to get out to the beach that was often closed in summer because another piping plover had hatched on the National Seashore.

But owning a camp also meant you had to accept the economic penalty of working year round on the Cape. It meant your kids might not go to quite as good schools as summer kids. It meant never having a summer vacation in another part of the country, but to stalwarts like Bob, these were minor sacrifices for the privilege of living as a close family on the edge of the Atlantic. Who knew the ultimate worth of growing up knowing how to operate your own boat or the worth of time spent exploring the outer beach to see what the ocean had brought in the night before?

Robert Crowell.

Bob knew he was a dying breed. His sister had moved to Sandwich and his brother worked in New York. They only used the camp for a week or so every summer. He was the only family who had been willing to pass up more lucrative jobs to continue his ancestors' Cape Cod traditions. He was the only family member still fully committed to Camp Crowell.

Bob remembered when the there were 300 feet of beach in front of the camp. You had to walk through a variegated landscape of dunes and swales just to get to the ocean. Now you could throw a stone from one side to the other. Almost every year these nor'easters eroded more sand off the dunes and washed water back into the marsh.

But on Monday morning Bob woke to a totally changed world. The waves still thundered against the dunes and Carol Scott's camp had been knocked off its foundation and would have to be burned. Water sluiced through the overwash and into Pleasant Bay. The only other person on the beach was Paul Fulcher who drove down to inspect the damage. The Orleans Superintendent of parks warned Bob that the backside road had washed out but at low tide he could probably still drive down the beach in front of the dunes. The waves had battered down the dunes between North and South Village, but by low tide most of the water had soaked back into the beach and the overwash was still dry.

Bob listened as the Boston Marathoners discarded their clothes as they ran up Heartbreak Hill, then regretted it when they reached the top and were hit by cold ocean winds still blowing through the city. He secured his boats and waited for low tide, luckily one of the lowest of the month. He dug out his truck and proceeded to carefully zig-zag up and down the foreshore to avoid the pounding surf. Finally he finished the five mile drive through soft sand back down the outer beach to the mainland in Orleans. His, would be the last vehicle to drive across this stretch of sand ever again.

Chapter Two
The Wager

April 24, 2007

Not much happened after the storm. It had carved steep cliffs into the dunes on Nauset Beach. Orleans and Chatham closed the area to all vehicles. For at least two weeks camp owners would have to get to their camps by boat. Pochet was still covered with mud and standing water and would have to dry out before being passable again. The closest you could get to the North Village overwash was across the bay in Chatham half a mile away. Onlookers gathered at Scatteree Landing, to gaze in awe at the surf as it towered over the camps on the outer beach.

At this point, ten men with shovels could have conceivably rushed to the beach at low tide and built up a four foot ridge of sand to seal up the break. But they didn't, and storm waves riding on top of astronomically high spring tides continued to push a broad plateau of sand into Pleasant Bay.

All the reigning geological experts confidently predicted that this process would continue and the breach would fill back in. Part of the problem was perception. People still like to think of a beach as a static entity—sure it changes after a storm, but then it appears to rest quietly until the next perturbation.

Ten men with shovels could have filled in the overwash when it first opened.

In 1976, Graham Giese, dean of the local geologists who study Cape Cod erosion pulled together a series of historical charts that chronicled the evolution of the Chatham barrier beach system. They revealed a 140 year cycle where Nauset Beach grows longer and thinner past Chatham, until it constricts the flow of water in and out of Pleasant Bay. The constriction restricts the tides so they built up a head of hydraulic pressure between Nauset Beach and the mainland at Minister's Point. High tide waters then want to find a quicker exit to the ocean, so when a random storm like the Patriot's Day Storm creates a washover it provides a convenient detour, and the out-flowing waters find a new exit. The inlet then migrates as much as six miles south until it reaches the same spot as it was 140 years ago, a new inlet forms, and the cycle repeats itself.

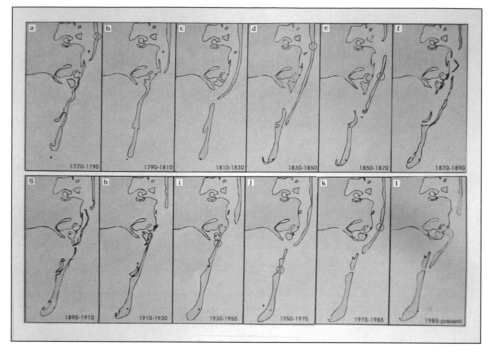

Graham Giese's 140-year cycle.

When I helped make a film about Pleasant Bay for the NOVA Science Series on public television, we put all of Graham's charts together and made an animation showing the cycle in a series of jerky segments that changed every twenty years. But the animation presented a misleadingly episodic looking record of the inlet and barrier beach cycle.

Instead of 200 years of charts made every twenty years, what we really needed were four hundred years worth of photos taken in the summer and winter every year. If we had animated those photographs in rapid succession it would have revealed that a barrier beach is actually a pulsating, quivering, animate being. The beach and dunes rise and fall with the seasons and with increasing and decreasing sea levels. Pseudopods of sand ooze into shoals behind inlets until suddenly the entire beach rolls over on itself moving ten or twenty feet closer to the mainland. This migration is even easier to see along the Gulf Coast of the United States where sea levels are rising faster, the land is compacting, and the continental shelf is shallower. There, barrier beaches migrate as fast as a hundred miles a century, almost a mile every year.

The realization that barrier beaches move is a recent notion, until the 1970s coastal geologists thought that barrier beaches stayed in one spot until they gradually eroded away. Now we realize that barrier beaches are not so much static geological features as they are just patterns of organization within a flux of energy. The sun translates its energy into wind, waves and storms which constantly build up and flatten down barrier beaches and cause them to migrate shoreward like slowly moving waves. When sea levels are rising fast, like they are at present, barrier beaches are low and flat and roll over more quickly toward the mainland; when the sea level is rising slower as it was for decades before the present, barrier beaches bunch up, build dunes and slow their shoreward migration.

Three hundred year-old tracks of a salt marsh hay wagon. Several hundred years ago this marsh was growing inside the outer beach. Since then, Nauset Beach has rolled over itself revealing this fossilized remnant of a bygone era.

Since the last time an inlet formed in Chatham in 1987, the sea level has risen three inches and Nauset Beach has moved almost 120 feet closer to the mainland. This happened episodically during major storms, but every tide also gradually deposited sand continuously into shoals inside the old inlet. Together, the two forces, one obvious and one less perceptible, built up energy for the next big change. Tides were being slowed by the shoals and restricted between the barrier beach and the mainland at Minister's Point. The water had to go somewhere, so, when the Patriot's Day storm provided a convenient detour, the system found its new exit.

Episodically thinking experts assumed that the inlet that opened in 1987 had initiated the next 140 year cycle of inlet migration. Actually, it had only been by chance that the 1987 overwash had occurred so far south. If it had occurred off Minister's Point in 1987 it probably would have created an inlet half a mile further north. In other words, the 1987 event had actually been a false start; the new cycle had not really been ready to begin until the overwash occurred off Minister's Point. Cape Cod had actually been living in a twenty year reprieve without ever having been aware of the fact.

Paul Fulcher was not so grounded in such episodic thinking. Unlike the shore-based geologists, the Orleans Superintendent of Beaches had been able to drive down to observe the overwash every day since the storm. Of course it was part of his job, but he also did it out of pure curiosity. Fulcher grew up surfing on Nauset and had been fascinated with waves. As a kid, he always seemed to be the first to know where the new surfbreak would form. In his bones he knew that waves were just patterns of organization within a flux of energy. Offshore bars, coarse-grained sand, an imperceptible bump or curve in the beach would cause the surfbreak to appear in a new location.

Perhaps it was this intuitive appreciation of energy that made Paul dubious of the experts' predictions. Like a true scientist he had made a point of going out every day to see for himself, and what he saw had confirmed his suspicions. On Monday water simply seeped back into the beach at low tide. On Tuesday it scoured a tiny little channel of water that continued to trickle back into the ocean at low tide. By Wednesday the channel was three feet deep and the overwash fifty feet wide!

Today, Paul had a chance to make some money on his intuition. Graham Giese had called to see if he could get a ride down the beach to see the overwash. They met at the Nauset Beach parking lot in the early morning and proceeded down the still ravaged beach. Paul liked the genial scientist and ribbed him gently about getting so much ink in the local papers.

"So where do you think this storm will go down in history, Graham?"

That was a damn good question. The recent Patriot's Day Storm certainly hadn't been as powerful as either the "no name storm" or any of the hurricanes in the 1950s, and it packed far less punch than either the 1958 and 1978 Nor'easters. But it had occurred when the sea level was half a foot higher than during those earlier storms. Plus, it occurred at exactly the wrong time. Winter storms had already lowered the barrier beach in several vulnerable points. To make matters worse, the Patriot's Day Nor'easter had hung around through several cycles of high course spring tides. It had not been a particularly powerful storm but it had caused what Graham called a "super overwash situation."

Paul waited quietly until they reached the North Village Overwash to spring his trap. He suspected that Graham already knew it was too late. The pattern of organization had shifted. The flow of energy had moved to a new phase of existence. Writers could write, experts could opine, and men of action could push for change, but nature was making it clear that a new cycle had begun.

Paul purposefully had not told Graham how much water he had seen going through the inlet the week before. He could sense the scientist's discomfort. He had already been quoted in the papers, how could he back down now?

"So Graham, how about a little wager?"

Graham laughed.

"Say about a hundred bucks that the inlet will stay open?"

Graham winced.

"How about a cup of black, hot coffee instead?"

Dr. Giese was silent driving back up the beach. Why had he been so damn positive in his earlier quotes? Now he would have to make a 180 degree turn in full view of the public. But that was part of being a scientist, you had to admit you were wrong in the face of better evidence.

"So what do you think about this idea of filling in the break?"

"Oh God, I don't know how I'm going to handle that one."

The new Inlet off Minister's Point.

Chapter Three
"Throwing Out the Baby with the Bath Water"

July 31, 2007

The day after the inlet broke through in April, Gerry Milden ran into Donald St. Pierre at the local Citgo station.

"Hey Donnie, see what those goof-off greenies have done to us now?"

It was a standing joke between the two men. For years, St. Pierre had collected money for the Massachusetts Beach Buggy Association's annual effort to put old Christmas trees and snow fencing on the low part of the beach between North and South Villages. This was where people used to land their boats and wear down the dunes walking to the ocean. But in 2004, the Cape Cod National Seashore made the MBBA remove the trees saying they were interfering with mother nature in the form of nesting plovers.

Gerry Milden had always seen the fencing as nothing more than cheap insurance. For a hundred bucks a year you could feel a little more secure that the ocean wasn't going to break through the beach and into your Minister's Point living room. But now the break had occurred, and Gerry was pissed.

"Whadda ya think we should do, Donnie?"

"We should just go out there with a front end loadah an' fill 'er in."

"You know that's never goin' to happen!"

"Well, maybe we should just get the Feds to do it for us."

The local lobsterman knew what he was talking about. Ever since Congressman Studds had attached a rider to a 1992 treaty with Estonia, the Army Corps of Engineers had dredged Chatham harbor. The first President Bush had been so eager to sign what would be the first treaty with a breakaway republic of the Soviet Union, that he had been willing to overlook the tiny additional item of funding.

"You know Donnie, that might just work."

The following Saturday, Gerry invited several neighbors to his house, overlooking what was rapidly becoming "the new inlet." The group decided that Dick Miller should be their point man. Dick had worked on several town committees, was active in the Provincetown Center for Coastal Studies and had helped start the Pleasant Bay Alliance. He was almost eighty and widely respected in town. He also came up with the name for their nascent organization, S.O.S. or "Save our Shores." It was an unfortunate choice. It was uncomfortably close to "Save our Sound," a controversial group of wealthy landowners who had shamefully stalled the construction of a wind farm on Nantucket Sound because it would interfere with their waterfront views!

But Dick was also an inside player. By June 7th he had helped Studds' successor, Bill Delahunt organize a meeting of every local, state, and federal office that would have to give permission to fill the inlet. It was at this State House meeting in Boston that the first of many red flags started to flutter. The superintendent of the Cape Cod National Seashore, George Price, made it clear that it was National Park Service policy not to interfere with nature in such matters. The Service had determined that one of the most important roles of barrier beaches was to act as buffers to protect the mainland. The beaches could only do this effectively if left alone so inlets could form and sand could migrate. Because so few people lived in national seashores, the park service could take this principled stand, that inlet formation and beach migration should be protected as natural phenomena. They had also discovered that inlets make compelling tourist attractions. People would drive hundreds of miles to view nature making such massive changes to the face of our planet.

"But," George stressed, "even if the park service could be persuaded to make an exception to this policy, it would take over a year to complete the necessary environmental impact studies."

Ted Keon groaned. The head of Chatham's Coastal Resources Department had already calculated that it would cost 2 million dollars to fill in the inlet, a year's wait would put the price well over 4 million bucks. That was starting to sound like real money.

Several days before the State House meeting, the Pleasant Bay Alliance held a forum of experts to explain the impact of the new inlet. Brian Howes had emphasized that the new inlet would help reduce the nitrogen loading in Pleasant Bay. Orleans selectman David Dunford's ears had pricked up at the news. Towns like Orleans had been dragging their feet on coming up with a plan to meet the state's targets for nitrogen removal. Nitrogen gets into groundwater from private septic tanks then travels underground to pollute estuaries like Pleasant Bay. The town had been balking at the idea of building an additional water treatment plant or sewering the entire town to replace the old system of private septic tanks. The inlet might at least buy the towns some time, if not provide them with a cheap way out of their dilemma.

The day after the State House gathering, the Chatham selectmen voted to hold a special town meeting so voters could decide on three articles. One, should the town raise $150,000 to study the new inlet; two, should the town borrow money to fill the inlet; and three, should the inlet be filled regardless of where the money came from?

This was when the dominoes really started to fall. Orleans and Harwich wrote letters registering skepticism over the wisdom of filling in the inlet. The Pleasant Bay Alliance wrote a long technical letter detailing all the ways the inlet would help improve the bay's water quality. Eventually even Chatham's board of selectmen and all the town's committees came out against the proposal to borrow money to fill the inlet, but came out strongly in favor of the article to study it.

Gerry Milden hadn't had so much fun since retiring from putting on trade shows. The man clearly knew how to juice a crowd. Soon he had the press swarming all over the controversy. The day before the special town meeting, Gerry ran into Dick Miller. Gerry was worried about the octogenarian, he looked haggard and spent. Both had been targeted by internet blogs running aerial shots of their multimillion dollar homes. Gerry had bought his home for $750,000, but the value of waterfront property had skyrocketed in the past twenty years. Richard had already put his house on the market, hoping the sale of this, his only major asset, would support him in his old age.

"Richard, Richard, my boy. Don't look so glum. You'll see, we're goin' to get the highest friggin' attendance of any meeting ever held in this town!"

"Yeah I know Gerry, and all of those people will be voting against us!"

The night of the meeting was unseasonably hot and humid. Huge air conditioners were blowing cool air into the Chatham high school gym several hours before the first people arrived. By 7p.m., the makeshift auditorium was jammed with over 600 residents, journalists, scientists and people simply there to make their feelings known. Most could not vote, but where were you going to find more entertainment on a mid-summer's night in July? As the crowd fanned themselves with information sheets, the democratic process unfolded.

Ted Keon was caught somewhere in the middle. The head of Chatham's Coastal Resources Department had been an early proponent of filling in the break. He was beginning to understand this prevailing New England penchant for leaving nature alone, but it still felt like fatalism to the native of Philadelphia. Keon had been a former planner for the Army Corps of Engineers and knew that you could use techniques like dredging and beach nourishment to work with nature to close inlets. Most of all, he knew that he was going to face some huge headaches if the inlet stayed open.

Chatham was fortunate to have such an experienced and well connected employee. But tonight Ted was in the uncomfortable position of having to explain that filling in the inlet was indeed doable, but the price had risen from $2 million dollars to $4.1 million dollars. Audible gasps filled the heavy night air, then the head of the finance committee rose to intone,

"This inlet was orchestrated by Mother Nature, and it's not nice to fool with Mother Nature."

When the applause died down, Richard Miller rose to state the obvious, "We recognize that support for filling in the inlet has eroded. The tide, if you will, has turned, therefore I humbly request that this article be indefinitely postponed."

This was where the meeting came unglued. People were confused. What did indefinite postponement really mean? Could the proposal be snuck back in at a later date? Better to just turn the old man down and make their feelings known. Voters had their chance when the main question was called.

"All those in favor of the town's borrowing $4.1 million dollars to fill in the inlet say 'aye.'" Two defiant voices answered from the back of the auditorium.

"Those opposed?"

Six hundred "no's" responded like a wave of rolling thunder.

"This is not going particularly well," thought Keon to himself. Now it was his turn to argue in favor of raising $150,000 to study the inlet so the town would avoid the chaos that ensued after the 1987 inlet. He detailed all the ways the new inlet would affect the fin and shellfish industries, how higher tides would affect the town's beaches and landings, and how many people stood to lose their homes on the mainland and along the outer beach.

"We have a multiyear problem ahead of us, and this study will provide a road map to give both local officials and homeowners guidance on dealing with all the changes facing Chatham Harbor and Pleasant Bay. Plus, the majority of the board of selectman and all the town's committees have come out in favor of doing this study."

But then the lone dissenting selectman rose to his feet. Sean Summers had already ridiculed Keon several times in public for predicting that the inlet would close, now he was at it again. First he quoted Orrin Pilkey, a coastal geologist who had made a career of denouncing coastal homeowners whose houses had just washed away.

'"How does one study such things when the input data constantly changes?' I think this study is a total waste of money!'"

Before anyone could rebut, someone called for a motion to cut off debate. The moderator was caught off guard. The meeting quickly voted in favor of the motion and then went on to defeat the study 388 to 204.

Ted Keon was floored. They had just defeated the article with absolutely no debate. Whoever had called for closure had done the town a grave disservice. Many suspected the call for closure had been planned well in advance of the democratic meeting.

But the voters were not yet through. To top off their sentiments that it wasn't nice to fool mother nature, they closed the meeting by voting a non-binding resolution saying they were against filling in the inlet even if federal, state, or private money could be found. Fred Jenson gave voice to the reigning sentiment of the night.

"If it's not a good idea to fill in the inlet with our own money, then it's not a good idea with state money either."

It had cost the town $1,500 to hold the special town meeting, but voters left the gym feeling satisfied that their voices had been heard. But cooler heads were dismayed. Voters had been manipulated into throwing the baby out with the bath water. It was clear to people like Ted Keon that the town was going to have to make some very difficult decisions and now they would have to make them without the benefit of scientific data. But why worry? It was something the White House had been doing for years.

The "Shoe Camp" wrapped in fog.

Chapter Four
The Shoe Camp Incident

August 9, 2007

It is midsummer, but Pleasant Bay is wrapped in a cold wet blanket of fog. Our world is constricted to a boat length of visibility within a diaphanous void of gray vapors. I am standing in the bow of Ethan Daniel's boat alternately wiping rain off my glasses and looking for the next buoy. If we miss one we could be swept through the inlet into the open Atlantic, not an appealing prospect in a twenty foot boat in the fog.

Suddenly I see what looks like a giant sunfish sculling below the surface, then I realize it is only an eelgrass covered lobster pot being pulled under by the six knot current. In fact we are in a vast field of lobster pots. Fishermen have learned that the prized crustacea have discovered the protected and now cooler waters of Pleasant Bay.

I still can't see any navigational buoys but we must getting closer to the inlet. Ocean going waves and strong currents are pulling us rapidly over the treacherous shoals. This half mile plateau of spreading sand is the flood tide delta formed by the incoming tides. It is mirrored by the ebb tide delta spreading out to sea. Both deltas are dangerous places to be. In early spring a lobster boat almost cracked its hull when an ocean wave slammed into the hard sand at the throat of the inlet.

The incident reminds me of the time I tried to traverse the 1987 inlet in a thick fog. I had a Boston-based camera crew aboard so I was trying to mask my concern as we puttered along what I thought was a direct line across the inlet. But it seemed to be taking an awfully long time. Suddenly I heard surf, but it was on the wrong side of the boat. Oh my God, I had taken us through the inlet and now we were about to be pounded to bits on the outer beach. But then a house loomed out of the fog above us. I had been concentrating so hard on not being swept through the inlet that I had been unconsciously cheating the boat toward the right. Now we were half a mile across the bay and about to be smashed against the rock revetment below the house. Try explaining all this on camera, while feigning the nonchalant air that you know precisely what you are doing, and exactly where you are going!

This time our biggest fright came when the giant, horselike head of gray seal popped out of the fog, then watched our sputtering passage with her dark, all-knowing eyes. Behind the seal a large fishing boat was parting the mists of fog, trawling for clams. This was also not a good sign. Sea clams are supposed to live on the outer beach. The final apparition to plague our day was a beautiful woman clad in white walking in front of us. Fog muffles sound and disorients vision... but a woman walking on water?

Finally it sunk in. She was walking on the spit of sand curling off the south side of the inlet. We had reached the new island created by the inlet when it broke off the southern end of Nauset Beach last April. Even in such a dense fog this new island attracts visitors On a good day there might be as many as 50 boats anchored in the protected cove behind the sandspit. The people quickly disperse along the nearly two mile length of beach newly devoid of noise and beach buggies. Many come to view migrating birds, others to make mischief in the warm protecting sands of the dunes.

Birds have an uncanny ability to realize the benefits of such a new island. We can hear the feisty cries of terns as they dive into the inlet and return to feed their chicks lined up along the water's edge. The chicks already know how to fly, but have yet to master all the intricate skills necessary to hover, plunge, and retrieve a wriggling sand eel. Instead the chicks fly to the shore to make their parents' flight that much shorter. Such efficiencies provide a crucial advantage to species that live so close to the edge. A new island devoid of predators and so close to such a productive source of food can make the difference between raising a single chick or two, a critical advantage in the lottery of life called evolution. No wonder they have adapted brain mechanisms to realize the benefits of both islands and inlets. These two new resources are made all that much more productive because they form an ecotone, an edge environment that is more productive than either the open ocean, an estuary, or fresh water environments by themselves.

The island is even more crucial to a pair of endangered piping plovers feeding in the swashline of the returning waves. Seven pairs of the diminutive birds nested on the beach this summer. That was a significant percentage of all the plovers nesting in New England in 2007. The new island's recently eroded beach provided the ideal habitat for the finicky bird's nests and it was newly cut off from plover crushing beach buggies. But most of all, the plovers were out here because they instinctively knew that an island will have fewer predators than the mainland. Unfortunately that is not yet true. It appears that a small rodent or skunk has destroyed five of the nests. But it will only be a temporary problem. Mammals need water to survive and they will eventually die off as the island's sources of fresh water dry up and the predators are unable to retreat to the mainland.

Further down the beach an oystercatcher snips the abductor muscle of a mollusk it finds on the shore. It is as quick as a skillful surgeon. It must be. If a mollusk closes down on its bill the oystercatcher risks being drowned in the incoming tide.

The oystercatcher stands amidst a flock of sanderlings, sandpipers, and semi-palmated plovers, also here to gorge on the billions of interstitial animals living between the surf washed grains of sand. They are also benefitting from this productive new island. But I have to admit I have a hard time telling all the birds apart. I am told that it is alright. People trained in marine biology have license to separate their birds into big brown birds, little brown birds, and owls!

The following day we returned to the inlet. A high pressure system had nudged the fog back out to sea and the sky was a brilliant cobalt blue. It was difficult to imagine how disorienting the fog had been only the day before.

Now it was easy to see the lobster pots and seals, and avoid the treacherous delta shoals. This time we landed on the north side of the inlet and made our way over the dunes to the ocean. It was a disconcerting sight. Ocean waves were ripping along the shore tearing great chunks of beach grass out of the dunes. Tangles of wild roses were being swept south in the grip of fast moving longshore currents. We could see where researchers had placed measuring sticks every ten feet in from high tide, most had washed away. The inlet was already 2000 feet across and growing wider at the rate of almost a hundred feet every week. The inlet was expected to double in size before it came into equilibrium with the volume of water flowing in and out of Pleasant Bay.

A beach camp perched precariously in the dunes only sixty feet from the mean high tide. This was the Achilles camp and it now enjoyed some of the most spectacular views in the United States. One window looked east over the Atlantic ocean, another south at the seals surfing through the inlet, a third looks west across the shallow waters of Pleasant Bay. Unfortunately the views would only last for another few weeks. The high tides were advancing twenty-five feet closer every week. The National Seashore was trying to decide how to remove this classically picturesque little camp before it is was swept into Pleasant Bay. Their options were few. They have already used the single permit granted to them by the state to burn the Scott Camp. For a while they considered giving the camp to anyone willing to cart it away, but their lawyers warned them that it would appear unseemly to get rid of federal property so quickly and for so little cash. The most efficient method would certainly be to just let it be known among the neighboring camp owners that Achilles was about to be destroyed, so they could take whatever they wanted. Achilles would be gone in a single weekend. Unfortunately most of the building would probably end up in the makeshift bulkhead of the next camp down the shore.

We fell into conversation with a fisherman trying his luck in the inlet. He showed us the waterline on his father-in-law's camp left by the 1978 storm. Every spring the Harrisses had to dig five feet of sand away from their Seamore camp just so they could open the door. The camp is one of the most beautiful on the beach. It boasts a cupola that allows you to look out over the ocean, the inlet, and the bay. In 1920 this camp was on the southernmost point of Nauset Beach. Since then, the beach had grown six miles south until the 1987 storm broke the bottom third off the barrier beach. Now the camp is back on the end of North Beach, once again.

The camp had been jacked up and placed on pilings after being undermined by the 1978 storm. But since then sand had buried the old pilings and was threatening to bury the camp.

The Harriss Camp, also known as "The Shoe Camp."

The Harrisses might have to apply for permission to put the camp on even higher pilings.

But the camp has another distinction. During the depression, a cargo ship filled with shoes ran aground off Nauset Beach. Locals came down that night to help rescue the survivors. But the following morning not a single shoe could be found. A week later an insurance adjuster discovered the camp packed floor to ceiling with "salvaged" shoes. No one ever came forward to explain the strange phenomenon. Ever since the camp had been affectionately known as simply, "The Shoe Camp".

Donald Harriss invited us in. It was a cozy camp. The walls were covered with clippings of past storms. Four teenagers were busy washing breakfast dishes and finishing a puzzle. There was no electricity or running water and they slept tooth by jowl on the second floor, but you could see they were loving the experience. The family regaled us with tales of camp living. Most revolved around catching and preparing food. Bushels of flounder could be jigged and frozen in spring. At least a hundred-fifty bass were caught each summer and scallops were scooped off the flats in the fall. Steamers were so plentiful they had become an item of exchange. If a neighbor dropped off some fresh fruit from the mainland he could expect a bushel of clams to appear on his back porch the next morning.

The Broad's camp, situated between Achilles and the Shoe Camp, lay on slightly lower ground. A foot of water washed inside the camp during the 1978 storm and three feet during the "no name storm" of 1991. Russell Broad received permission to build a bulkhead after the 1987 storm. It had not pleased the neighbors because, while it had protected the Broad Camp it had also increased erosion in front of the Harriss camp. But no one had complained, that was not the way on the outer beach where you only had fifteen neighbors in your entire village. But now the tables had turned.

At the same time the ocean was tearing away at the dunes on the outer beach, longshore currents were moving the equivalent of a football field filled eight feet deep with sand down the Nauset system every month. Formerly all that sand flowed six miles down the beach to build up the end of Nauset Beach, now it was sweeping into Pleasant Bay. It had already built up the flood and ebb tide deltas, but something else was happening as well. Waves were sweeping around the recurved spit on the north side of the inlet then refracting off the Broad's bulkhead and dropping their load of sand on the shore in back of the Harrisses' Shoe camp. Their bayside beach was growing inches thicker with every tide. The beach glistened with the purplish red color of its semiprecious garnet grains. The grains were an indicator that the sand had been dropped by high energy waves because garnets are heavier than the white silica sands that made up the adjoining beaches. Both minerals came from the granite cores of northern New England mountains that had been gradually eroded and transported here by past glaciers.

The implications were clear. Although the inlet and outer beach are eroding, the inner beach was thickening with every tide. If the Harrisses were lucky, they would soon have several hundred feet of new beach on the bayside of their camp. If they could get permission to put their camp on pilings a hundred feet closer to the bay, they might just be able to enjoy their camp for another generation. The same can not be said for the Broad and Achilles camps only a few feet away.

Chapter Five
The Attack

August 11, 2007

It was the end of another long hot summer day on Nauset Beach. A lone gray seal surfed the five foot waves rolling through the new inlet and across the broad plateau of sand stretching half a mile into Pleasant Bay. As the currents carried the seal swiftly over the sun-dappled bottom his large eyes saw a dizzying tableau of sand, crabs, and scattering minnows. His five hundred pound bulk flashed quickly overhead gulping great mouthfuls of sand eels. The five inch long Ammodytes had forsaken the safety of the sand to forage for plankton on the incoming tide. A school of them dashed over the edge of sand into a deep channel of swaying green eelgrass. But a large striped bass lunged out of the depths to devour them. It was a fatal mistake. He never saw the dark shape of the seal as it plunged over the lip of the growing sandbar to capture him.

A lone Gray Seal.

The sand eels were one of the first species to discover the new inlet with its concentrated supply of plankton. They were followed by the gray seal Halichoerus gryphus, or "the hook-nosed sea pig." The entire herd of several hundred seals had moved north from their old feeding grounds off Monomoy to feed on the shoals of sand eels sluicing in and out of the new inlet. The male seal preferred to feed alone in the inlet, but now it was time to rejoin the rest of the herd sitting safely on Lighthouse Beach.

The tide had started to slacken, and the rays of the setting sun now were entering the water at a low, oblique angle. With the changing tide and setting sun, the seal had lost the advantage of both speed and light. His vision was specially adapted for daylight hunting. Besides he had eaten over seventy pounds of bass and eels. His body glistened with more than enough fat and blubber to carry him through the upcoming breeding season when he would be too busy coupling and competing with other males to gorge himself on eels.

The seal swam slowly out of the inlet and into the inky green waters of the Atlantic. Here he turned south to swim parallel to the shore to join the rest of the herd now sunning themselves quietly in the fading light on Lighthouse Beach. But something was wrong. The water was deathly quiet. He no longer heard the comforting clicks of small fish feeding on the bottom. He looked into the gloom, but his daylight vision failed him. The advantage had shifted to his enemy lurking almost motionless and invisible against the bottom.

The Great White Shark had lain in ambush just beyond the inlet for half an hour. She had heard the muffled laughter of surfers overhead, but they were not her favored prey and too close to shore. Now, when the long dark silhouette of the seal appeared above her, the shark was ready. Muscles along the caudal peduncle of her tail powered her skyward. Nicitating membranes slid in place to protect her eyes during the coming attack. She rolled back, opened her mouth and the full force of 5000 pounds of rasping skin, cartilaginous flesh, and a mouthful of inch-long serrated teeth slashed into the seal's vulnerable underbelly. The impact of the blow threw the seal into the air and he fell back into a cloud of his own frothing red blood. The shark swam back toward the bottom and waited. She had severed several arteries in the seal's unprotected belly. Better to wait for the seal to weaken before attacking again. The last thing she needed was to have an eye gouged out in the death throes of a large, potentially dangerous prey animal that was going to die anyway. The shark could smell the cloud of blood billowing toward her and feel vibrations of the seal's still vigorously pumping heart. But she knew its struggles would soon be over.

When it was clear the seal was too weakened from loss of blood to fight back, the shark circled in for the kill. She tore three great mouthfuls of viscera and blubber out of the still twitching animal then abandoned the carcass. She was not really all that hungry. She had just enjoyed the hunt off her newly discovered inlet. Onshore a group of surfers looked in horror. They had been in that same water only moments before. The only partially eaten carcass would wash ashore the following morning.

After feeding, the shark dove back to the bottom and continued to swim slowly south. Was this the same young female shark whom fishermen had seen thrashing around in a Monomoy tide pool three years before? A few weeks after she had blundered into the tide pool she had accidentally gotten herself caught in a tidal creek on Naushon Island thirty miles away. This was the same creek where well-tanned summer kids used to tie ropes to the Naushon footbridge and water ski on the powerful currents of the outgoing tide. Evidently this accident prone young shark just loved shallow water, fast currents, and, perhaps, people. She received more than her dose of all three as she stayed stuck in the shallow pool for two weeks while photographers paid entrepreneurial Woods Hole fishermen a hundred bucks an hour to ferry them across Vineyard Sound to take pictures. On Naushon, state and federal officials would only allow them to get within a hundred feet of the shark as she quietly cruised about her little pond.

Normally it is only human celebrities who get such paparazzi treatment. But this young shark had picked up this curious new behavior of swimming close to shore to explore creeks and tide pools. Perhaps she liked the attention, undoubtedly she enjoyed the food. It was much more abundant and easier to catch near shore. The roguish behavior had its benefits as long as you didn't mind spending a few weeks in a pond having hundreds of people take your picture.

But this was not the first time a shark had developed such behavior. During the 1930s a Bull Shark started to wander in and out of shallow creeks along the Jersey shore. There it attacked mostly young children swimming in the warm protected waters. For several weeks the entire East Coast was transfixed as the shark killed swimmer after swimmer during a summer of terror. Sound familiar? Peter Benchley used the incident as the basis for his best seller, "Jaws."

But was this really the same shark that had blundered into a Monomoy tide pool three years before, then been seen attacking seals off Monomoy last summer then Nauset and Lighthouse beaches this summer? Do we have another rogue shark? Did we help create it through bringing back seals and allowing her to become habituated to humans when she was trapped on Naushon? We will never know! Just before scientists coaxed the shark out of her brief captivity on Naushon Creek they jabbed a tag into her tail. The last thing they saw as the shark swam back into Vineyard Sound was the tag caught in a bed of eelgrass.

A blue shark feeding on butterfish

Chapter Six
"Driftwood"

Labor Day Weekend 2007

Throughout the summer Russell Broad fought the sea to save his home. A friend gave him scraps of wood and the butt ends of two by fours from his family-owned lumber yard. Russell would load these into his boat and carefully ferry them across Pleasant Bay to "Driftwood," his summer camp on Nauset Beach. Once on the beach, Russell hammered endless rolls of snow fencing into the dunes, strung together wooden pallets to extend his bulkhead, and packed energy soaking eelgrass behind the pallets to protect the narrow bank of sand between his camp and the rising waters of Pleasant Bay.

Russell's father had built the bulkhead after the 1978 Blizzard flooded their camp. For years it had provided the Broads with a sense of security. While beside them the Harriss camp rested only a few feet above high tide, "Driftwood" sat securely behind its solid wooden bulkhead.

But something changed after the April storm. The beach in front of the Harrisses' camp started to grow. Each wave would wash up the swashline, lose energy and deposit a thin filigree of purplish-red sand onto their beach. The darker color of the sand indicated that it was made up of tiny semiprecious garnet crystals which are heavier and require more energy to move than the more abundant grains of silica sand. By the end of summer, the garnet sands had thickened the beach, so that now a broad plateau of new sand protected the Harriss camp. But, the same waves, only a few feet away, slammed into the vertical face of Russell's bulkhead, then ricoheted off, still retaining their energy. Instead of dropping out to build up the Broad's Beach, their sand stayed in suspension and moved downstream to build up the Harrisses' beach. Waves were already tearing away the dunes on either side of Russell's bulkhead, and had started to undermine the narrow bank of sand behind.

Russell could see that his bulkhead wasn't working. In fact it had become a textbook example of why bulkheads don't work. Yet Russell couldn't stop himself. His father had built this bulkhead and to remove it seemed like giving the waves an invitation to invade his home.

Russell's family gathered to support him. His daughter made a point of bringing her kids to the camp as often as she could. Laurie had first heard about the break when she was on vacation in California. Just hearing her father talk about "Driftwood" brought tears to her eyes. The simple camp had been part of their family for three generations. It was central to who they were, how they thought of themselves as a family.

There were no phones, no computers, no lists of things to do, no ferrying of kids to endless activities at "Driftwood." It was simply enough to sit in the sunlit kitchen with Grandpa and Grandma watching the kids play at the water's edge. Fortunately, Tim loved the camp as much as Laurie and, of course, their three children adored it. Nothing lit up their faces so much as hearing that they were about to spend a weekend at Driftwood, nothing except the news that it would also be a "cousins weekend."

Laurie thought that Driftwood would be in their lives forever. She remembered helping her grandmother plant endless plugs of beach grass into the dunes to protect their camp. She remembered her grandfather making bonfires on the beach and setting off fireworks on the Fourth of July.

Since this could be their last summer at Driftwood, Laurie and her brothers made sure to get to the camp for many weekends as possible. Tom had flown in from California just so his kids could see their cousins over the Fourth of July weekend. The weekend had become something of a family tradition. Laurie had only missed two Fourth of July weekends in all her 39 years and those had only been because of her best friends' weddings.

This Labor Day was going to be their last, long, bittersweet weekend of the summer. The weather was gorgeous and they did all the regular things; swimming, boat trips, collecting sand dollars and lucky stones for the upcoming school year, digging steamers for their last supper on the beach. As the fire dwindled and the embers glowed, Laurie finally had a chance to catch up with her mother.

"I'm worried about Russell. He's been working so hard on that damn bulkhead, I'm afraid he'll get a heart attack."

But Laurie had never seen her father look better. His arms were well muscled and tan. Sweat dripped off his forehead and he had that certain fire in his eyes she hadn't seen in years. It was the fire of Santiago fighting his mighty fish, Ahab battling the Great White Whale, perhaps even King Canute trying to stop the tides.

It had been a good clean fight, up until they had received that letter. It had come from the Chatham Conservation Commission, telling Russell to stop repairing his bulkhead. It was dated the day after the National Seashore had torn down the Achilles camp. Russell was sure the rangers had ratted on him.

The Conservation Commission was well within their rights to tell Russell to cease and desist. They argued that his wooden pallets would break away and become hazards to navigation. But the letter had done another thing. It had robbed Russell of his dignity. It was one thing to fight a good fight and lose to nature. It was another to be told you couldn't do anything to protect your home.

And of course, the letter produced exactly the wrong results. For the last few days, Russell had been considering removing the facing on the bulkhead on the slim chance that the waves might start building up the beach faster than the tides could tear it down. It would have been a gutsy move, and it might even have worked. But the letter changed everything. Now Russell knew had to change his strategy to fight this new, faceless, human enemy.

A man could use his hands to fight a good clean battle against nature and lose with his dignity intact. If the ocean won, so be it. He could go to his grave knowing that he had fought the good fight and lost. But to lose because your hands were tied behind your back by some penny ante bureaucracy? That was the kind of defeat that could kill a man's soul, and gnaw at his innards for eternity.

But, perhaps it didn't really matter in the end. It seemed almost inevitable that if Driftwood wasn't flooded out by the rising waters of the bay, she would be washed away by the ocean. The Atlantic was already tearing great chunks off the dunes that protected the camp to the east. Wouldn't it be kinder to just let Russell fight his personal battle against nature, than to tie his hands behind his back for a few more agonizing months?

A dory above beds of blue mussels.

Chapter Seven
The Wreck

September 5, 2007

Immediately after Labor Day weekend the winds shifted abruptly north. It was almost as if the weather knew that summer was officially over. It was too cold to dive so I decided to take one last summer look at the inlet. The tide was so low we had to land on the less interesting south side. But I casually mentioned to my daughter, Chappell, that this was okay. There was an old piece of wood lying partially buried in the sand that might possibly be part of a shipwreck. We had ignored the graying timber on previous trips thinking it just a random piece of driftwood. Besides there wasn't enough intact material to identify the timber even if it were part of a wreck.

I can't claim to be wise enough to know when to wield the awesome power of reverse psychology, but I did know my teenage daughter had always loved archeology and was in the process of writing a story about ships and pirates. While Ethan and I anchored the boat, Chappell wandered off in search of the piece of wood. I mentioned to Ethan that this was our first really boring day on the inlet, the tide was low, there were no seals, no swift current, no rushing waves. Chappell probably thought the whole thing was a crashing bore, all this nonsense about erosion and inlets, just her Dad caught up in another one of his strange new obsessions.

When we found Chappell she was on her hands and knees intently brushing sand off the timber. She had already discovered it extended 15 feet further than the three feet of exposed driftwood we had ignored before. She had also located some wooden pegs called trunnels and two iron bolts used to attach timbers to adjacent pieces of wood. The tops of the bolts had a distinctive squared off shape. Now this was potentially significant; you could possibly use this detail to date the wreck. Soon all of us were on our hands and knees intently brushing away the sand. Not only was the timber attached to other pieces of wood, but they extended deep into the sand. We reburied the artifact, cell called to the proper authorities, and resolved to spend the next day in the archives of the Chatham Historical Society.

Chappell Sargent brushing sand off the timbers of an old wreck.

The last time these timbers had been part of a full blown ship appeared to be on December 23, 1896. A vicious Northeaster had stalled off Cape Cod, lashing the outer beach from Provincetown to Monomoy. Clouds of roiling snow and sheets of piercing sleet cut visibility to a scant few feet.

Winifred Nickerson was repairing some gear in his fishing shack on the Chatham shore. Suddenly the naked masts of a schooner loomed out of a slight break in the squalls. She was hove to just off the outer bar. In an instant, Nickerson knew the ship was in serious danger. He had spent five years in the Life Saving Service and knew that the patrolman from the Orleans station had probably missed the distressed schooner on his five mile patrol to the end of the beach. Now he would be heading north again to arrive back at the station in time for the 4 p.m. watch. Nickerson exhorted the small knot of fishermen that had gathered to catch another glimpse of the vessel.

"We got to get out theah. That vessel will be in ten thousand pieces before mornin'. It may be our only means of savin' life."

"Now take it easy Winifred. There's time enough to go in the mornin'. If we go over theah now, we'll have to stay the night, for we sure as hell can't find our way back after dark in this kind of a storm!"

Much to Nickerson's dismay, the group decided to meet again at 7:30 to see if the storm hadn't abated enough to try again. Winifred promised that if they were successful, he would walk the 5 miles up the outer beach to alert the Orleans station.

"Meanwhile. I intend go straight to the Chatham office to see if I can't wire the Orleans Station. Any of you boys willin' to come along?"

Two hours later the two men arrived at the Chatham telegraph office, only to discover that the cable that ran underwater to the Orleans Life Saving Station had parted two weeks before. But the operator wired the Highland Lighthouse observer in Truro who in turn found an open telephone line to Amelia Snow, operator at the Orleans railroad depot. Amelia promised to find someone to hand deliver a message to the superintendent of the Massachusetts Life Saving Service who lived in Orleans. The first person she called was the owner of a local livery stable.

" No, I am sorry, Amelia, but I wouldn't send one of my horses out in such a storm for love nor money."

A young man offered to take the message to Superintendent Sparrow for $5, but since nobody was willing to guarantee the money, he demurred and went home. The local expressman said he would gladly deliver the message to Superintendent Sparrow, but he had to wait for the incoming train. It was already two hours late because of the storm. Finally, Henry Cummings volunteered to go. Aided only by a sputtering lantern the young Orleans businessman arrived at Sparrow's house at 11 p.m. Benjamin Sparrow rang up the keeper of the Orleans station at once.

"Keepah Charles, this is Superintendent Sparrow. This is rather a wild goose chase, but we have a report of a vessel in distress. We don't know where the vessel is, and we don't even know that she is yet ashore."

"Well, we have to go out but we don't have to return, do we?"

Superintendent Sparrow laughed in spite of himself. Both men knew this was the motto of the United States Life Saving Service.

"I'll break out the beach apparatus as soon as my two surfmen return from their patrol, superintendent."

"Good, I'll join you as soon as I make my way out to the station."

"We do appreciate that, sir."

By 10:40 Keeper Doane of the Chatham Life Saving Station started receiving reports from his patrolmen that pieces of wreckage were coming in on the surf. It was a sure sign that a ship was breaking apart in waters to the north. The south patrol found a yawl missing its hull from its bow to the centerboard box. Had its occupants been swept overboard as they tried to escape the vessel before she broke to pieces? Further down the beach another patrolman found five hatches and a broken quarterboard with the letters, "Calvin B. Or—". This was even more frustrating. The surfmen knew that men were dying just beyond the breakers, but they couldn't reach them, and they couldn't even row across the inlet to alert the Orleans Station.

By the time Keeper Charles' two patrols returned to the Orleans Station shortly after midnight, an eight foot snowdrift had built up in front of the doors of their boathouse. Seven men had to shovel away the water soaked snow before they could wheel out the surfboat and hitch it to their single draft horse. For several more hours the phalanx of men had to shovel a path in front of the boat cart and try to locate the faint track that wound through the windswept dunes. They held wooden shingles in front of themselves to protect their eyes from the stinging sand and sleet. But several men suffered frostbite and Superintendent Sparrow lost his vision permanently from the lacerations he received that night. Despite the crew's best efforts, the horse broke down several times and had to be helped to its feet by the equally exhausted men. For the last few miles the surfmen were pushing the cart mostly by themselves.

At 2:25 the crew finally spotted the stricken vessel. She was four and a half miles south of the station and 600 yards offshore. Her four masts were still standing and anchors were holding her head into the wind, but her hull was already submerged. Breakers were rolling down the length of her decks. Nobody could survive in those waves.

The exhausted team rolled out a small cannon used to fire lines into the rigging so the crew could winched ashore over the breaking waves in a breeches buoy. But the Lyle gun was useless, The ship was too far offshore and there was no sign of people still lashed to the rigging anyway.

The beautiful four masted schooner that had once plied the oceans from Boston to China was helpless. Wave by wave she was being smashed to pieces on the outer bar. This had been the Calvin B. Orcutt, en route from Portland to Norfolk without cargo. She had hoped to make port before Christmas. Instead all seven of her crew members were lost. Frozen bodies washed up in the surf on Monomoy for a month after the ship went to pieces. The sailors had probably fallen from the rigging as they slowly froze to death. Two bodies were never recovered, and two were never identified. Ministers from all the Chatham churches officiated at the funeral of the unidentified men and their bodies still rest in unmarked graves overlooking the scene of the tragedy.

This part of the outer beach has a rich history of wrecks The earliest was the Sparrowhawk, a forty foot barque carrying colonists to the Virginia Colonies. It had gone seriously off course and grounded in Pleasant Bay in 1626. Governor Bradford from the Plymouth Colony had to lead a rescue expedition to the Cape and paddled across Pleasant Bay in a borrowed Indian dugout to retrieve the unfortunate survivors.

The richest wreck was certainly the Wydah, Sam Bellamy's pirate ship, that went down off Eastham with all the treasure from the seventeen ships of the Spanish main he had just captured. For years people told tales of gold doubloons that mysteriously appeared in the local Cape Cod economy. But nobody gave the stories much credence until Barry Clifford, a Martha's Vineyard boy who had paid attention to his grandfather's stories, retrieved the ship along with several hundred million dollars worth of gold and silver coins.

The wreck of the Calvin B. Orcutt affected history in a different kind of way. The Life Saving Service was severely criticized for its slow response to the disaster and the crew members inability to do anything once they reached the scene. The problem was not the unjustly criticized Orleans crew, but that this part of Nauset Beach was a magnet for wrecks. More vessels passed along this coast during the late 1800s than anywhere else in the world except the English Channel. On a fine summer day, Winifred Nickerson could sit on his front porch and watch over a hundred tall ships, packet boats, and fishing smacks sailing just beyond the Chatham bars. At least two other major wrecks, the Onondanga and the Orissa had grounded within a mile of the same spot the Orcutt had met her demise.

For our purposes the most interesting aspect of the Orcutt wreck was where she lay. She was not on the outer beach but inshore of the inlet. Records of the wreck stated that pieces of the wreck had been swept into the upper beach. But in 1896 the beach was about half a mile offshore from it's present location. This piece of the wreck had probably been swept up onto the side of the inlet that had opened in 1846.

When the Cape Cod Life Saving Stations had been built in 1871 they had been designed so they were eleven miles apart. Patrols would set out from each station then meet and exchange a metal disc at a halfway station before returning back to their own station. But there had always been a gap between the Orleans and Chatham stations because of the 1846 inlet. Patrols had to walk to the inlet then turn back. There was no direct communication between the two stations and a serious gap in protection.

In 1897, a year after the Orcutt disaster, The Life Saving Service built the Old Harbor Life Saving Station to fill in the gap. At that point the new station was on the southernmost end of Nauset Beach. As the inlet migrated south and the beach continued to grow, the station became a mecca for summer camps and eventually the dividing point between North and South village. By 1987 Nauset Beach had grown six miles further south, and Graham Giese's 140 year cycle had repeated itself. In 2007, the inlet had opened just south of the 1846 inlet, and exactly where the Calvin B. Orcutt had gone down just two days before Christmas on that frigid night in 1896.

The Old Harbor Life Saving Station at its original location on North Beach. It was moved to Provincetown by barge in the 1960s and is now the Cape Cod National Seashore Visitor's Center at Race Point.

Chapter Eight
Fieldwork

October 16, 2007

"O.K. you guys, get your butts off the gunwales. Remember what happened last time?"

Ted Keon was sporting the beginnings of a new beard, so the self-described city boy could fit in with us natives. But we quickly complied with his orders. Mark Adams, geologist with the Cape Cod National Seashore, stowed his yellow GPS system under a tarp to protect it from the spray blowing in over our port bow. As Ted used a recent aerial photo to guide us through the shoals and quickly ebbing tide, Jim Gallagher, Chatham's assistant conservation agent, moved aft, and Graham Geise and I had time to catch up.

You couldn't help but like Graham Geise. He still retained the southern drawl and cultured style of his Tidewater, Virginia, background. I first met Graham at the Bermuda Botanical Gardens. We were on the first leg of an oceanographic cruise to Africa, South America, and the Baltic. I remember being impressed that he seemed to know the Latin name for every tree and tropical flower we walked by. I met Graham again at the La Paguera Biological station in Puerto Rico. He and Stormy Mayo were hatching a plot to create The Provincetown Center for Coastal Studies, so Stormy could study whales close to the source, and Graham could continue his research on the geological history of Cape Cod.

The outer arm of Cape Cod is without doubt the most studied barrier beach system on the planet. In the late 1800s, H. L. Marindin ,with the U.S. Coast and Geodesic Survey, hammered small brass markers into the cliffs of the Outer Cape from Provincetown to Chatham. In 1964, John Zeigler from the Woods Hole Oceanographic Institution relocated the old geological markers and used them to calculate the erosion rate of the Outer Cape. He discovered that the tops of the cliffs were eroding back about two feet a year, but they also could lose as much as twenty feet during a single storm. It was common to see houses teetering on the edge the cliffs, and both the Highland Lighthouse in Truro and the Nauset Light in Eastham had to be moved back to prevent them from tumbling into the Atlantic. Chatham's twin lighthouses had not been so lucky. They had pitchpoled down the bank after the Chatham inlet opened in 1864.

Graham had been John Zeigler's research assistant that first summer, and he grew to love their study area so much that he bought a house on High Head in Truro. High Head was where the prevailing Northeast winds normally hit the wrist of the Cape creating longshore currents that push sand north to build up Provincetown, and south to build up the 40 mile Nauset Beach system that supplies sand to Eastham, Orleans, and Chatham. Ever since Georges Bank slipped below the surface in the wake of the last Ice Age, this system has pushed the equivalent of a several dozen truckloads of sand down the outer beach every year. That is a lot of sand to build up beaches and fill in inlets!

Our inlet was fast approaching. While Ted held the boat steady against the current, we stripped down to wade ashore. The water was still surprisingly warm for mid-October. On landing Mark set out with his GPS to measure how much the inlet had grown. It was just a matter of clicking off coordinates from a satellite orbiting overhead. I missed the old days, only twenty years before, when scientists still had to wade into the surf to hammer in measuring rods, then watch them wash away.

The new inlet that opened in April, 2007, is in the foreground. The old inlet that opened in 1987 is in the background.

But Graham had such an intuitive feel for the dynamics of this beach that he used a more contemplative method. He would simply stroll down the beach, occasionally stooping to examine a handful of sand or kneeling to jot an observation in his ever present little notebook. While the rest of us only saw a beach, Graham noted where the beach was straightening slightly, or that wispy roots of beach grass jutting out of the foreshore indicted an area of new erosion. He was like an artist noting details of light before rendering the entire scene. Yet he was still amazed.

"There is just an incredible amount of sand coming in here. I'm just not sure where it is all coming from."

I was astounded at the changes that had occurred since my last trip only than a month before. Waves had knocked a hole the size of a truck through Russell Broad's bulkhead. A month before we had to climb up a rickety ladder to clamber over the bulkhead. Now you just had to walk through the bulkhead and up a sandy slope into their camp. There was a large shallow depression where the Achilles camp had been. It looked like a wisdom tooth had been extracted from between the dunes. All that remained of the camp were the tops of the pilings that had been driven twenty feet into the dune to anchor the structure in place. The Seashore had removed the camp just in time. Ocean waves were lapping at the spot where the southern porch used to be. The ocean side of the beach had taken a beating as well. Russell's snow fencing was lying in a battered ball in the surf and waves were now licking the dunes only thirty feet above his camp. It looked like Driftwood was only a single Nor'easter or a month of regular erosion from disaster.

But as we circled back to the boat, things started to look better. The equivalent of a football field worth of sand had swept around the spit to the south of his camp. A month ago these waves would slam directly into his bulkhead at an acute angle, then ricochet off, keeping their sand in suspension. Now, so much sand had swept over the spit that the waves were sliding almost parallel to the face of the bulkhead and had started to drop their sand. Perhaps the hole in the bulkhead had allowed the waves to lose some of their energy as they washed up the sandy slope they had already created behind the bulkhead. Whatever the reason, two feet of newly deposited white sand was now piled along the face of the bulkhead, where only a month before, the waves had been undermining the structure. Now that the process had started, it looked like it would quickly accelerate, giving Russell a ray of hope on his forward flank—despite the impending disaster to his rear.

By the time we finished our survey, the tide had dropped so we could clamber back aboard the boat and putter across the inlet's momentarily slack waters to the south side.

This side held even more surprises. The south side of the inlet was actually migrating north into the inlet, an eight foot deep sandbar, the length of two football fields curved back 200 meters into the bay. Waves and currents were eroding the south side of the inlet, straightening the outer beach slightly, and pushing the sandbar back into the inlet. Winds had blown so much loose sand over the beach that it had reburied the remains of the wreck my daughter had investigated only a month before. Most of all, we were impressed with how much sand was sweeping into the inlet and we remained mystified about whether more sand was coming from the north during northeast storms, or from the south during southeast weather.

However, what was eminently clear, was that the incoming sand had built up a rich new environment. We could see the foot-long tracks of hundreds of dime sized sand dollars as they inched their way up the lip of the flood tide delta and into the now incoming tide. A horseshoe crab lay beside them perhaps waiting to move offshore for the winter.

We were impressed with how much sand was sweeping into the inlet.

It was clear that the inlet was still getting wider but the process had slowed down and the channels on either side of the inlet were not necessarily getting any deeper. But the thing that bothered me most was the future. You could almost walk cross the inlet at low tide. All you would have to do was wade through the shallow channel on the south side, walk dry shod around the perimeter of the flood tide delta, then take a short swim across the north channel. It was difficult not to get the impression that the ocean wanted to fill in the inlet. At least six football fields worth of sand, filled eight feet deep, had flooded into this inlet since April.

On the way back to the dock I asked the scientists if they thought the inlet might close on its own. It was clear the question made everyone a little uncomfortable. The week after the Patriot's Day storm, they had all been quoted saying that the inlet would close. At the special town meeting, only three months later, they had said it would cost $4 million dollars to fill in inlet artificially. Now, if they turned around and said it looked like mother nature was going to close the inlet in after all, it would look like the experts didn't really know what was going on. Graham spoke up first.

"Well, soon after the inlet opened, I did think it would close up pretty quickly. It looked like it would simply fill in, block itself up and close. That still seems to be the case, and yet it remains open. Clearly there is more to the operation of this system than I understand."

Graham went on to explain that both the north and the south inlets were now competing for dominance. During high tide, water was flowing into the bay through both inlets, but during low tide most of the water was still exiting through the old south inlet. Most importantly, there still appeared to be more than enough water flowing through the old inlet to scour it and keep it deep and open.

Whether you thought the new inlet would close, really depended on whether you thought the 1987 inlet had been a fluke. Graham explained that he thought it had not been.

" Prior to 1987, I assumed a new inlet would open opposite Minister's Point as it had done in the 1600s, 1700s and 1800s. But it turned out that most of the constriction had really been because of shoals building up in the throat of the pre-1987 inlet opposite Lighthouse. That is why the 1987 inlet stayed open and got deeper and developed so quickly. But now we still have that healthy inlet to the south so the new north inlet is not getting deeper."

He continued to explain that under natural conditions waves should have eroded the mainland opposite the 1987 inlet to relieve the head of water pressure. Instead, homeowners had built revetments which had constricted the throat of the inlet between the mainland and the inwardly migrating outer beach.

In other words, the revetments had been responsible for the new inlet that opened a mile and a half north of the old inlet. This was not an argument you would want to make in public.

But I still didn't really have an answer to my question. Then I remembered an incident that had occurred to me when I was covering the Montserrat volcano in the Caribbean. The Montserrat Volcano Observatory had just published a press release stating that there was a forty percent chance that the volcano would erupt, a forty percent chance that it would go dormant, and a twenty percent chance that it would stay the same. I asked the head of the observatory how he had possibly arrived at such precise numbers.

"Oh dat was very easy. I locked five experts into a room and told them I wouldn't let them out until they told me if they thought the volcano would explode, stay the same or go dormant. Two said it would explode, two said it would go dormant, and one said it would stay the same. Voila 40 percent, 40 percent and 20 percent! "

You might be surprised how many times such methods are used to arrive at such scientific sounding numbers. When I returned home I e-mailed Ted, Graham, Mark, and Jim.

"Do you think the inlet will stay open, close, or that the two inlets will stay in equilibrium?"

I won't say precisely what each scientist and science writer wrote, but I will tell you that when all the votes were tabulated we arrived at a sixty percent chance that the inlet would stay open, a twenty percent chance it would close and a twenty percent chance it would stay the same. There it is, that aura of numerical certainty. Almost as good as, "four out of five doctors recommend Robitussin for their own families!"

Chapter Nine
Donald Harriss

October 26, 2007

It is 2:30 a.m. The pockmarked face of the full moon hangs above me, almost twice as large as normal. This is not an optical illusion. The moon is thirty thousand miles closer to the earth than it was during the Patriot's Day Storm, and closer to the earth than it will be all year. This is the October perigean moon, the largest full moon of 2007.

A perigean moon glides through the tide charts like the bulge of a pig moving down a python. When it comes in contact with the straight line alignment of the sun, moon, and earth, you have a perigee-syzergy tide. Put them together and you have a twenty point scrabble word, a proxigean tide. They only coincide every fourteen months, so they will occur in January one year, two months later in March the next and two months later in May the following year. It is during such proxigean tides that our coasts experience their worst flooding.

This perigean moon, which Indians called the Hunter moon, is the reason I am driving to Lynnfield, Massachusetts, at such an ungodly hour. I had expounded on proxigean tides in an e-mail to Donald Harriss. Now, you might expect that an 86 year old grandfather, who had recently lost his wife to cancer and was facing knee surgery might feel a little despondent to hear that his house might topple into the sea. But Donald would have none of it.

"So Bill, are you up for an adventure? If you can get to my place by 4 a.m., we can drive down to the Cape and be on the beach by low tide. I should have enough time to close up my camp and you should have just enough time to take your pictures before the high tide drives us off the beach."

How could I refuse? The time passed quickly as we cruised beneath the deserted streets of Boston and on to the quiet roads of Cape Cod. Donald kept me entertained with stories about his father who bought their camp; and his wife, six kids, and several generations of grandchildren who had all loved it. It was clear that the camp influenced everyone's lives. One daughter was practicing maritime law and a son-in-law was making environmental films. Donald's children were scattered all across the country, but they still kept an eye on the camp, and their father, from a camera mounted in a house on Scatteree landing.

After we let just enough air out of the tires, Donald shifted into four wheel drive and we started lurching down the six and a half miles of barrier beach to his camp. Most of the time we drove on a broad shelf of sand between the ocean and the dunes. Donald explained that we were driving on the remains of the summer beach. The beach was still wide and the sand was still firm. But winter storms would soon eat away the beach, leaving only a narrow strip of soft sand below the dunes, "It's almost impossible to drive in that stuff."

When the waves started lapping at our wheels, Donald had to shift into reverse and back down the beach so we wouldn't get trapped between the tide and a berm of sand that was too steep to climb. Several times we had to meander back and forth between the rutted trails behind the dunes and firm packed sand of the outer beach.

But soon we arrived at the camp just in time for a beautiful, clear, but chilly sunrise. It was low tide, so five foot waves were still pounding the lower beach and a brisk wind was blowing so much sand off the dunes I had to protect my cameras. We had to shovel several feet of sand away from the door, before so we could open it. I remarked to Donald that he kept a "Cape Cod key," one hidden, either directly overhead, or under the nearest door mat.

"Everybody does that out here. Then, if somebody gets stranded in a winter storm they can either find a key or break just one pane of glass to get into the camp for the night. We also keep enough food inside so that a person can have something to eat while they are waiting to be rescued."

I caught Don quietly picking up a stone and slipping it into his pocket.

"What's are you going to use that for, Don?"

"Oh that," he said, "You see, every time I come out here I collect a pebble and bring it back to put on Evelyn's grave. She loved it out here. Afterwards, I usually take a few minutes to tell her how the camp is, and what we all did. She died much too young."

While Donald started taking down family photos, I used the remaining time to walk around the point before the incoming tide could catch me between the ocean and the dunes. I could hardly believe the changes that had occurred from just a week before. Waves had torn ten more feet off the dunes. At first I didn't realize that the remains of the old middle road where Russell Broad used to park his beach buggy were gone. You could still see where waves had flooded into the cavity left by the Achilles camp but soon even that cavity itself would be erased. The erosion had unburied several pieces of the Old Harbor Life Saving Station and the cable that connected it to the Orleans station back in the 1800s.

Four foot piles of sand rested in front of Russell's bulkhead on the bayside of the beach. But it was clear that the locus of erosion had moved downstream. Now waves were by-passing the bulkhead and eating away at the shelf of garnet sand in front of Donald's camp. But the most arresting feature was a narrow spit of sand jutting east off the flood tide delta. It was only forty feet from the shore aiming directly at Fred Truelove's camp. The spit had already slowed the currents in the channel leading to the inlet. In short order it might push the channel closer to Donald's camp or start diverting the outgoing tide around the flood tide delta and back down the western side of the bay to the old inlet, a mile and a half distant.

Back at the camp, I tried to stop Donald from crawling through an upstairs window to the roof outside.

"Here let me do that. You don't want to hurt your knee!"

"Oh, no. It doesn't matter, I'm goin' to get a new one on Tuesday anyway."

We continued to remove more books from the shelves and haul furniture into the attic to escape the expected flooding. Donald removed two sweaters that one of his daughters had knit for his father, but that everyone had loved to use after he was gone.

After we put heavy wooden shutters on all the windows and doors, Donald called me outside.

"Hey Bill, come on out here, someone wants to take our pictures."

Had a photographer driven to the end of the beach to take picture's of the camps demise? All I could see was Donald talking on his cell phone.

"Brian says wave!"

Finally I understood, Donald's son, Brian was sitting at his computer in Atlanta looking at two blurry, but still distinguishable blobs, waving their hands at an invisible camera mounted half a mile away in somebody's living room window on Scatterree Landing in Chatham! Later, Brian Harriss sent me the photos and I finally realized how close we had actually been to the waves breaking all around us.

After a quick lunch, we went outside to witness the highest normal tide of the year. But before we set off to walk around the point, Donald decided to move his beach buggy. It was a prudent move. Waves were already spilling over the tops of the dunes and washing under our tires. It was clear this narrow shelf of beach might not be here after the high tide.

It seemed like a sacrilege to walk through the dunes that were doing their best to protect his home. But Donald said, "It's like my knee. They're goin' wash away anyway, so we might as well walk through 'em one last time. But I must admit, it's a little like watching your favorite dog die."

For almost an hour we watched the waves methodically batter down the dunes guarding Russell Broad's camp. Waves were breaking over the tops of the dunes, and rushing down toward his house. It was clear the water would soon be flooding into his first floor, and in a month, a steady flow of water could be washing directly through his house from the oceanside to the bayside.

Five-foot waves were rushing past Russell Broad's camp.

Donald figured that his camp would also be flooded, but that after the flooding was over he might still be able to put his camp up on pilings. I could see where a surveyor had already marked the place on slightly higher ground where he hoped to move his camp. He explained that the last four camp owners on the end of the beach planned to all hire the same pile driver to save money.

But something on the ocean side of the beach made me uneasy. About five hundred feet north of where we had parked the car I could still see the broad shelf of the summer beach. Waves were breaking against the well developed berm of sand.

But here, where we were standing, the berm was gone, and waves were slamming directly into the dunes.

Gradually it dawned on me that I was using the wrong metaphors to understand this system. I had been so concerned with currents, waves and the volume of water sluicing in and out of Pleasant Bay that I had lost sight of the big picture. The southern section of the beach was not acting like a normal barrier beach undergoing rollover. The beach was acting as if someone had just flipped an hour glass, and now sand was running out creating a funnel shaped depression. And we were standing in that ever-widening depression! This meant that almost a quarter of mile of the southern end of the beach was going to flood into the inlet. Instead of just the Achilles' camp being lost; perhaps the Achilles', the Broad's, the Harrisses', the Truelove's, and several more camps might wash away. It was a chilling revelation. I didn't want to mention my concerns to Donald until I had checked them out with some experts.

That evening we drove back in silence. Donald had a quick nap. He had a dinner date and a few more things he had to do before his knee operation. I just wanted to get home to catch up on my sleep.

The next day my panel of experts confirmed my worst fears. The southern portion of the beach was indeed going to continue washing through the new inlet. That realization led to a new concern. There was nothing to say that another storm wouldn't cause an overwash further up the beach. Whether the new break stayed open, depended on how deep the bay was behind the beach, as much as whether there was another inlet further south. If the bay was deep behind the beach the inlet would act like a tall hour glass and the inlet would stay open. If the bay was shallow from former overwashes, the inlet would act like a short hour glass filled with too much sand. The sand would clog the bottleneck and stop flowing. The inlet would close.

It seems that the most important responsibility the owner of a barrier beach has is to maintain the beach so the hour glass wont turn over. For once an inlet opens the ocean can attack houses on the mainland. This was not just an academic argument. For years the owner of Nauset Beach, the Cape Cod National Seashore had let groups like the Massachusetts Beach Buggy Association maintain the beach. In the 1990s they changed that policy because they felt snow fencing would interfere with the ability of nesting endangered birds to get to their feeding grounds. But now their new policy was jeopardizing the homes of hundreds of their neighbors both on the barrier beach and in the bay behind. If a new inlet opened further north hundreds of new houses would be affected. And one of those houses was mine!

Rogues and patterns.

Chapter Ten
Rogues and Patterns, Patterns and Rogues

Hurricane Noel
November 3, 2007

When you think you have finally figured out one of nature's patterns, she has a habit of throwing in a rogue, just to keep you humble. After finishing my previous chapter on inlet formation, I paused to read the morning papers. Hurricane Noel had already killed 148 people in the Caribbean and was in Florida, downgraded to an extratropical cyclone, but still packing plenty of punch and accelerating rapidly north.

I loaded my cameras, packed my bags, and rented a car before realizing it would be foolhardy to drive to Cape Cod in hurricane force winds. Besides, I could probably learn just as much watching television in my warm house in Ipswich than driving to Chatham in the teeth of the storm.

I set up my situation room in the attic. One computer carried e-messages from the members of our far flung camera crew, another carried images from the inletcam on Scatteree landing, and my television was tuned to the Weather Channel's Mike Bettes, reporting from the Chatham Fish Pier.

I watched the Weather Channel all day. They were excellent

at giving you the big picture. They had crews stationed on the beaches of Florida, North Carolina, New Jersey, and Montauk Point where fishermen were hauling in huge striped bass, made hyperactive by all the oxygen churning around in the storm tossed, supersaturated waves.

But the Weather Channel was frustratingly lax at presenting details. Here they were, stationed in Chatham and they seemed totally unaware of what was really significant. All they were showing were moored fishing boats bobbing around in slightly choppy seas. Our own inletcam was transmitting far more compelling images. Although the shots were rainswept and blurry, you could see that the Harris and Broad camps were still standing, but surrounded with ever rising waves. I even tried to call the Weather Channel headquarters to see if they wanted to use our inletcam, but found there was no way to reach an actual human being in Atlanta on a Saturday morning. I wonder how many tips they miss by not having someone available to take calls during weekend emergencies.

Sunday morning, I awoke, again, at 4 a.m. This time it was to drive to Plymouth, to join the rest of our camera crew. Susan Haney had spent all day filming Noel in Scituate and Bob Daniels was recovering from a bumpy flight back from D.C. We convened over coffee at Dunkin Donuts and decided to drive to the Chatham airport to see if we could hire a small commercial sightseeing aircraft to fly us over the beach. If that didn't work, we would drive on to the Fish Pier to see if we couldn't find a boat. If all else failed, we could always drive to Orleans and hitch a ride down the beach in a four-wheel drive vehicle.

I started to get an inkling of what our day was going be like at the airport. The flight operator had put his planes into a hanger the night before, and now the power was out, so he couldn't open his hanger door.

"With 50,000 people without electricity, I don't think it's likely we will be back in business anytime soon."

Ted Keon wasn't in his office. A cop we flagged down on a side street scrolled through his cruiser's computer readout and told us no beach patrols were scheduled for the entire day. A news crew at the Lighthouse overlook said they had already given up on trying to get to the outer beach. I was beginning to think I had led everyone on a wild goose chase, the entire day was going to be a bust, and an expensive one at that.

Things finally started to improve at the Fish Pier. Another camera crew was filming the top of the Broad's house, half a mile across the harbor. But Russell's roof was not on Russell's house. It had been washed a mile down the beach and was now lodged beside a grounded fishing boat. A recreational boat had also been swept through the inlet and into the open Atlantic, but then had been swept back in twenty foot seas and 85 mile an hour gusts, to come to rest on the foot of South Beach. Noel had come much closer to Cape Cod than anyone had expected.

I flagged down the assistant harbor master's boat. He agreed to take us to the outer beach to snap a few pictures.

"But it has to be a quick tour. The tide is falling, and there is so much sand in the water you can't see if there are any new shoals."

It was a small step in the right direction. We leapt at the chance.

As we approached the shore I could see that the Broad's house was scattered in several pieces, but the Harriss camp was still upright.

But my attention was really elsewhere. There were several people scouring the beach. I yelled across the water to see if anyone could give us a ride back down the beach. But nobody could hear. There was only one solution. I apologized to Susan, stripped to my skivvies, and waded ashore. John Kelly was amused at my audacity.

"Sure. We have a few more things to do in our camp, but if you promise to put your clothes back on, I'll drive you to Orleans in my pickup."

Under the circumstances, it was not a bad deal at all.

The harbor master dropped us off and I finally had a chance to inspect things more carefully. It was totally disorienting. I couldn't tell where Russell's two-story camp and boat house had formerly stood. The foundation was almost in the water, the kitchen was lying on the beach, the boat house appeared to have been swept toward the ocean while the main house had crashed into the bulkhead, broke apart, and was swept into the bay, where it lost its roof.

Donald's house was still standing, but canted over toward the ocean. The kitchen had been torn off the old part of the camp and stood upright in the sand. The tattered flags, that all the camp owners used to announce they were in residence and safe, still fluttered from the ceiling over the cooking utensils which still hung from the wall as if nothing had happened. Beside them, was the refrigerator, still upright and attached to the wall, holding shelves stacked neatly with clean plates.

Donald's camp was still standing, but canted over toward the ocean.

It was the refrigerator that made me into one of the most loathsome creatures on the face of the planet—a looter. My back was still aching from the morning drive and I had an aspirin in my camera bag, but no bottled water. There was the refrigerator. There was my pill. I opened the door, and sure enough there were all the rows of unopened ginger ale cans. It didn't even fizz, when I flipped open the first can. I swallowed my pill and turned to offer a quiet toast to Seamore Nickerson and the four generations of Harrisses who had all loved this camp.

The rest was not a pretty sight. All the chairs and rugs that Donald and I had carefully put on tables the week before were scattered through the shell of the ravaged camp. Most of the central chimney had tumbled down, and lay in big blocks of bricks on the sand covered floor. Gas lanterns still hung from the walls and a forlorn little sign hung outside marked this as, "The Seamore Camp, circa 1896."

Don's well head and hand pump were still in place, but sticking out of the sand on the lower beach instead of in the dunes. The ocean had eaten away seventy feet of dunes in front of Fred Truelove's camp, eighty feet in front of Donald's camp, and ninety feet in front of the Broad camp. The depression in the hour glass was getting wider and steeper. All that sand had actually narrowed the inlet and deposited more than ten feet of material in front of the remains of Russell's bulkhead. The current was slack, a teapot and a toilet seat lay, side by side, in the quiet waters of the bay.

The Broad and Harriss camps had been destroyed by two rogue events; the Patriot's Day Storm that had opened the inlet in April, and the remains of Hurricane Noel that had delivered the coup de grace. In actuality, however, Noel had really just speeded up the process of inlet formation. The two camps would have washed away anyway, in only one or two more months of the regular, inlet caused erosion.

Ultimately sea level rise is the engine that drives this pattern. The ocean has risen three inches higher than it was when the first inlet opened in 1987, six inches higher than it had been when Russell Broad's father bought Driftwood during the war, and a full foot higher than when Seamore Nickerson built the Harriss camp in 1896—rogues and patterns, patterns and rogues!

Russell Broad's boathouse was still standing because the ocean was able to flow in the front doors and out the back doors.

Chapter Eleven
Five Days in November

November, 2007

Things happened quickly after Noel. November 11th, found us at the Chatham fish pier waiting to film Rob Crowell at his camp on the inlet. It was a cool, brisk autumn day with strong winds and twenty foot waves. Half a dozen Coasties decked out in orange foul weather gear were also at the pier preparing to head out on a rescue mission. But they didn't seem to be in a great deal of hurry. I asked why they were going out. They only exchanged silent glances.

It seemed that the night before, a Boston-based fishing boat had been idling 23 miles off of Nauset Beach, waiting for the weather to clear. As soon as the sun rose they cast their net. On the very first haulback a deckhand saw a dead man lying amidst the flounder flopping in the cod end of the net. The rattled crew members had to throw out the fish, and lose another day's wages, because the Coast Guard ordered them to steam directly back to Chatham to unload their unwanted catch. This didn't seem like a very auspicious start to our day, to say nothing of the crew member's upcoming trip.

The cadaver was in pretty good condition, with its skin and face still intact, and only a single missing foot. Later we learned the body had been in the water since 2001. The dead man had been only one of two people who had been embalmed and given an official burial at sea in the past seven years!

On the outer beach, fifteen foot waves surged through the inlet. At high tide they started overtopping dunes to create a new overwash only a thousand feet from Rob's camp. It was too rough to cross to the north side of the inlet, but we could still see the remains of Russell's buildings being pounded by the breaking waves. The following day I was at home and had to settle for watching his camp be demolished on the inletcam. It was probably just as well, I had grown to like the entire Broad family and didn't particularly feature having to shove a microphone in front of their nose and ask how it felt to watch their house being destroyed. Hour by hour, I watched as a giant backhoe picked apart first their bedroom, then kitchen then boathouse, before dumping the lot into a construction vehicle to be hauled off the beach. By the end of the day all that remained was Russell's bulkhead still standing defiantly in the setting sun. The next day, that too had been pulled up and hauled away.

Chatham had lost five camps since the inlet opened only six months before. Yet, thanks to the summer's special vote, Ted Keon still couldn't tell homeowners what was going to happen in the near future. He knew the development of this inlet was already strikingly different from the 1987 inlet. By this time in the evolution of the 1987 inlet, ocean waves had already scoured 200 feet off the mainland, undermined two homes, and were poised to demolish the Galanti house, all on national television. That was another difference. You couldn't drive a TV van down Nauset Beach, so there hadn't been any macabre death watches as reporters dressed in city shoes waited for people to lose their homes. This time all the damage had occurred on the outer beach. The mainland had been largely spared. Ted knew it was because of a different pattern of inlet development, but didn't know exactly what that pattern was.

But that was also about to change. Ted had been able to cobble together $40,000 from the town, the Army Corps of Engineers, and The Alliance for Pleasant Bay. The Alliance could justify the grant on the grounds that it would help the surrounding towns figure out how much less money they would have to spend on nitrogen mitigation. It was not the $150,000 study that Keon had hoped for, but at least it was a start.

On November 8th, Ted had watched as a team from Falmouth Scientific deployed a wave and tide gauge, just offshore of the new inlet. This time they weighed it down with extra heavy weights, and attached a pinger so it could be located if it was swept out to sea, as had happened only a few weeks before.

On November 14th, Ted watched again, as a technician from the Army Corps of Engineers trailed a LIDAR system over the side of the harbor master's boat. LIDAR was like a policeman's radar gun, only in addition to radar it used a laser beam linked to three global positioning system satellites to map the bottom topography of each inlet. Data from both the wave and tide gauge and from the Light Detection and Radar system could then be combined to form a model of water flowing in and out of the two linked inlets.

In six months time, the model could be displayed on a color coded television monitor to show exactly how warm and cool water currents stream through the inlets during a normal tidal cycle. This would finally give Ted a reasonable idea of whether the inlets would stay open, close, or remain in some kind of dynamic equilibrium. It would not be a foolproof forecast, but it would certainly be more accurate than the quarter bets we had been placing against each other. It was not a full blown hydrodynamic and bathymetric study, but it was a start. Now Keon could at least describe the new beast standing at Chatham's door.

By November 16th the disposition of the Harriss camp loomed as an issue. Donald, still in bed getting used to his replacement knee, didn't want to make any hasty decisions. His camp was still upright and largely intact. He figured that as long as his camp stood, he would still retain his right to rebuild. His nephew had been taking bids to see if they could move the camp to higher ground, or put it up on pilings. The building inspector had another opinion. He felt the building was more than 50% damaged, a danger to the public, and should come down.

But there was another legal issue that went back to colonial times. Under riparian law, owners can only retain ownership of their land as long as it remains above water. As soon as it disappears below the surface it reverts to common tidelands or in the British parlance, "The Queen's Bottom."

This bit of arcanum meant that if Donald's land washed away he would lose ownership of it. Plus, when the beach started to grow south again in a decade or more, he could still not reclaim ownership. Legally, his land would become part to his neighbor's lot to the immediate north!

This had actually happened in the 1800s, when Seamore Nickerson could have been the beneficiary. In 1896 his camp was the southernmost camp on the beach. If he, and later the Harrisses, had pressed their claims, by 1987 they could have owned almost four miles of accreted beach from their camp south to opposite Monomoy Island! Seamore's relative Oscar Nickerson did this more successfully in 1924.

A similar case occurred more recently in South Carolina. In the 1960s, a weekend fisherman named M. A. Boryk bought a 25 acre plot of beach on the south end of Topsail Island. Mr. Boryk developed the land, and used the proceeds to put his kids through college. By the time he died, Mr. Boryk's beach had grown south and added 125 acres of new free land worth more than $30 million dollars to his heirs. Not a bad deal for a weekend fisherman with a fourth grade education!

You would think that in this modern day and age, when a high school student can plot out a lot of land with a handheld GPS system, the practice of surveying property according to landmarks would be obsolete. If Donald Harriss could determine his deed by coordinates on the globe instead of using landmarks, he could reclaim his land when it reappears with the growing beach. In the meantime the question remains, who was going to end up holding the last camp on the beach and be the beneficiary of the next 140 years of the Nauset cycle?

Chapter Twelve
A Day of Thanksgiving

November 24, 2007

It is November 24, the end of a long Thanksgiving weekend. The Nauset Beach parking lot has a strangely festive air. Carloads of surfers don shiny neoprene wetsuits to brave the freezing temperatures and ten foot waves. Several four-wheel drive vehicles, pause to take air out of their tires before heading down the beach.

At 2 p.m. we meet Russell Broad and transfer our photographic gear into his car. He has kindly offered to take us down the beach to refilm the aftermath of Noel. We have to drive through the remains of a large fresh water lake that closed the beach buggy trails after the hurricane. When a storm coincides with a high course tide it actually raises the water table under the barrier beach, and, since fresh water floats on salt water, the fresh water is the first to rise up through the beach creating large unnavigable puddles. I don't find it particularly comforting to know that, during a storm, this beach we are driving on is little more than a water infused slurry of sand. I am beginning to be very thankful that Noel appeared so suddenly that we hadn't had enough time to hatch any harebrained schemes to spend the night in a camp in order to film the offshore hurricane!

I am also thankful that we have a veteran beach hand like Russell to take us down the winter beach. He maneuvers us through a cut in the dunes so we can drive on the foreshore where the sand is more compact. Neophytes always try to hug the dunes to avoid the waves. One of them is in front of us now, frantically waving his arms. It doesn't look good. He is up to his hubcaps in a rut of unconsolidated sand. But we have three adults and a camera crew aboard, perhaps we have enough manpower to simply muscle his vehicle out of the newly eroded soft sand and down to the foreshore.

But the driver has flagged down the wrong car. We are be happy to help—in exchange for filming the entire embarrassing sequence. Six of us put our shoulders to the rear bumper and nothing happens. The wheels just spin deeper and deeper holes until the vehicle's chassis is hung up on a bed of sand. Russell uses his spare shovel to dig away more sand and we try again, this time in reverse. Millimeter by millimeter the heavy vehicle starts to move. Finally the driver is able to build up enough momentum to break out of the deep rut of sand and run down onto the hard packed beach.

As the camera continues to roll, we ask the driver if he had thought to bring a cell phone, shovel, or had even paused to take the air out of his tires. He insists that he had been driving down this beach all his life, but had accidentally left his cell phone on his motel dresser, and this was the first time in fourteen years he had headed down the beach driving without a shovel.

Suddenly it felt doubly good to be driving down the beach with an old beach hand like Russell. But ahead of us was a reminder that even old hands can get in trouble on a winter beach.

On December 16, 1963, Mercer Curtis drove his Land Rover to the tip of Nauset Beach before sunrise to shoot some ducks. But, by late afternoon he hadn't returned, so his wife put in a call to the Orleans chief of police.

"Chet, I hate to bother you, but Mercer went down to Nauset this mornin' and hasn't returned. I would've called earlier but he's been huntin' down there down there for 40 years, and knows how to take care of himself."

Landers hung up, and dialed his counterpart at the fire station.

"Larry, Chet here. Can you drive us down the beach in the department jeep? I expect the huntin' was good and we'll just find Mercer sittin' somewhere warm and cozy with a few extra ducks over his limit!"

The winter beach was so frozen Larry Ellis could drive in high gear and even get back into the dunes to some of the camps that you couldn't normally reach in winter. The chief of police and the head of the fire department searched every camp from Orleans to the end of Nauset Beach in Chatham. But there was no sign of life, no sign of the Land Rover, and no sign that any of the camps had been broken into. It was getting dark and both men were expected to attend town meeting later that night so they reluctantly turned around.

But, on the way back home, Larry made a slight turn and the jeep broke through the crusty surface and lodged in the soft sand below. After fifteen minutes of fruitlessly spinning his wheels, Larry stepped out to check out the situation.

"You know Chet, I think I smell some smoke and I swear it smells like wood smoke."

"I don't smell anything but your goddamn overheated gearbox, but you're the fire chief. If you say its wood smoke I say let's take a look."

The two drove back upwind following the faint trace of smoke drifting through the dunes. Suddenly Chet spotted the dim light of a kerosene lantern flickering in the window of an empty camp. A motionless body lay on the floor wrapped in a thin covering of wet blankets

"This is the Taylor camp. We musta missed it on the way down. We bettah break in and take a look."

The camp was freezing. Frigid winds had been blowing through the smashed window all day. A wood fire smoldered weakly in the stove. It was almost out, but it had done its duty, sending its tell tale scent out wood smoke out through the still night air and into the experienced nose of the Orleans fire chief.

Mercer Curtis was soaking wet, barely alive and comatose when they found him, but they were able to warm him up enough to hear his story.

Mercer had driven down Nauset before sunrise, and was turning his Land Rover into the foreshore to park when a rogue wave caught him broadside. The wave broke over the Land Rover, and stalled his engine. Just as the wave was in process of dragging him and the Land Rover back into the surf, Mercer jumped into the armpit-deep waters.

As his Land Rover disappeared into the surf Mercer started the four mile slog back up the beach in his heavy, wet hunting clothes. He broke through the crusty sand several times and wondered if he would be able to regain his footing and continue. But he finally spotted the low silhouette of the Taylor camp. The Taj Mahal couldn't have looked any more beautiful. He broke in, started a fire, put a lamp in the window and wrapped himself in blankets before losing consciousness.

If Mercer had omitted any of these steps, he would have surely died. If the Orleans fire department jeep hadn't broken through the crust precisely where it had, Larry Ellis never would have smelled the telltale scent of wood smoke. If Mercer's Land Rover hadn't washed completely away, the searchers might have assumed the worst and called off the rescue. Indeed the winter beach is not a place to be taken lightly. You might be only half a mile from downtown Chatham but you are thousands of miles from the comforts and safety of civilization.

When we reached the Harriss camp, I was again thankful that we had not decided to spend the night. The first time I saw the remains of the building, I thought the camp had stayed stationary and the garage and kitchen had broken off. This time I realized that the garage had actually stayed anchored in place because it had been filled with drifting sand, and the old part of the house had been lifted up and floated several feet toward the bay. It had only stopped because it bumped into two benches nailed to the boardwalk in front of the camp. Donald and I had sat on those benches only a two weeks before.

Inside the camp, we could see where the water had risen four feet above the floor. If we had stayed in the camp during Noel the roar of the ocean would have been deafening. People had heard it seven miles inland. As the water rose and the chimney toppled we would have retreated to the attic. Imagine how we would have felt as the entire building was lifted off it's foundation and was about to be dumped into the frigid waters of Pleasant Bay. We probably would have survived but I doubt we would have wanted to head back down the beach any time soon.

The following day we inspected the mainland. The tide had washed through a small marsh on Minister's Point and was lapping against a gravel topped road that led to half a dozen homes. This was a 5.8 foot tide, the highest of the year. After this peak of high course tides passed there would be no more 5 foot tides until well into 2008. This meant that at least one variable would be working in the homeowner's favor. Sea level rise drives the entire system, but homeowners can discount its effect on a yearly basis. For all practical purposes, rising seas only make a difference on a decadal time scale. The ocean was 3 inches higher during Noel than it had been during the 1987 storm that started this recent cycle of inlet formation, only twenty years before.

Tides and sea level rise fit into regular patterns that can be measured and forecast. But then there are the rogues; the storms, storm surges, waves, and winds that build upon these regular patterns and can raise the ocean thirty, forty, even fifty feet above normal. These are the variables that can't be predicted, but are crucial on a day to day basis, even deadly on an hourly time scale. These are the rogues that people in Chatham would grow to fear in 2008.

Global warming will lead to higher waves and more storms.

Chapter Thirteen
La Nina

December 7, 2007

In early December a mass of cold arctic air bulged south out of Canada to clash with a moisture laden front of low pressure sweeping north from the Gulf Coast. Snow fell from Minnesota to New York and thirteen people in eight states died in automobile accidents.

The low passed just east of Cape Cod as it had during Noel. Only this time, high tide was just over four feet, average for the Outer Cape. More dunes eroded on Nauset Beach. Every day on Dan Ryan's Inletcam I could see the profile of the barrier beach was growing ever flatter. At high tide, Russell Broad's former camp site was now completely underwater, meaning he was running the risk of losing title to his property.

Under normal conditions, this would have been only a moderate storm, causing little erosion. However, since the inlet opened, Chatham had become the canary in the coal mine for the rest of the country. A hundred years from now, it will be the bulwarks of Wall Street and the condominiums on Boston's Atlantic Ave that will be have waves lapping at their front doors. Two hundred million people will be in danger of being flooded out of their homes.

New Englanders have always loved to talk about the weather, but since the inlet opened, people in Chatham have become particularly vigilant. On a day-to-day basis you could safely ignore global warming, but you could never ignore the weather. Weather, however, is inextricably linked to climate change and the chains that link global warming to daily weather are climatic oscillations.

The best known climatic oscillation is the El Nino–La Nina cycle. During the El Nino phase, warm water spreads across the Eastern Pacific, sometimes for several years. This causes the jet stream to stay north, so storms march straight across the continental United States instead of dipping to the south. This makes the Northeast warmer and hurricanes more powerful, because they draw their energy from the Atlantic ocean whose surface waters are hotter during the El Nino phase of the oscillation.

However, during the La Nina phase of the cycle, temperatures are cooler in the north, Nor'easters tend to approach New England from the south, and there are fewer hurricanes in the Atlantic Ocean and more in the warmer Pacific.

There is a similar oscillation in the North Atlantic that caused the Little Ice Age in the 1600s and a South Atlantic oscillation that effects the frequency of East Coast hurricanes. During the wet phase of the South Atlantic oscillation the climate is stormier and wetter over Africa and this breeds more hurricanes; in the dry phase there are fewer hurricanes and the Sahara Desert expands.

During the 30 years from 1944 to 1960 the South Atlantic oscillation was in the stormy wet phase and 15 major hurricanes slammed into the East Coast of the United States. During the next thirty years, from 1960 to 1992, the oscillation was in its calmer dry phase and only three major hurricanes hit the United States. That changed again in 1996 and now we are back in a period of more frequent storms. We have already experienced over a dozen major hurricanes including Ivan, Charley, Rita, Wilma, and, of course, Katrina. Unfortunately, this phase is expected to last for at least another twenty years.

These oscillations are the key to understanding persistent weather patterns. Weather forecasters have done an admirable job educating the public that storm fronts travel west to east across the continental United States. Now they should do an equally good job informing the public about the importance of climatic oscillations to day-to-day weather. In the future, last weekend's forecast might sounded like this:

"We are still in the moderate La Nina pattern that started last winter in mid-January. Temperatures will continue to be below normal in the northern tier of the country and locally we will see thunderstorms on Monday. We can expect these la Nina conditions to last well into the first quarter of 2008.

"Now in sports. How about those Patriots? They seem to be in their own pattern of defeating winter opponents. How long can this dynasty last? Here's Mike Lynch with the sports. What do you say Lynchie?"

Of course, scientists would really like to know how global warming affects climatic oscillations. Will El Nino periods become longer and more intense? Will the patterns oscillate back and forth more rapidly as they have in past periods of global warming? Or, are we entering what energy advocate Amory Lovins calls a period of global weirding in which our planet will be convulsed in a patternless era of ever more frequent examples of weird weather?

As 2007 drew to a close, it was clear that Chatham had become a laboratory for studying how climatic oscillations and storms affect both inlet formation and coastal erosion. In 2007 we had both the Patriot's Day Storm in April and the remnants of Noel in November. Both storms were categorized as hundred year storms because of the amount of erosion they caused on the Outer Cape. If the world continues to emit as much carbon dioxide into the atmosphere as expected, cities like Boston and Miami will also experience an average of two such hundred year storms a year. Instead of camps being lost on Nauset Beach, condominiums will be washing off Biscayne Boulevard.

In the wake of a storm, sand smothers a bed of eelgrass.

It was also clear that we have entered a new phase of erosion on the fragile elbow of Cape Cod. Chatham had lost nine mainland houses after the first inlet opened in 1987, and so far four camps had been destroyed after the second inlet opened in 2007. During the summer months the barrier beach near the inlet was eroding an average of 25 feet a month. Since November it was averaging close to a hundred feet of erosion a month. It looked like the entire six miles of barrier beach could break up during the coming few decades and Cape Cod's vulnerable mainland would be exposed to the full force of the Atlantic. Most coastal areas will not see this sort of erosion until well into the next half century.

But Chatham would see even more changes in 2008.

The end of an era?

Chapter Fourteen
The End of the Year.
The End of an Era?

December 28, 2007

As 2007 drew to a close, I was witness to a series of surreal and interrelated events. On the island nation of Bali, UN delegates were locked in a stalemate on global warming. The European Union had proposed that nations adopt a goal of cutting their carbon emissions by 25% to 40% when they met in 2009 to renegotiate the Kyoto protocol in Copenhagen.

The sole holdout was the United States, who was threatening to torpedo the entire framework meeting by vetoing their allies' measure. The American delegation was booed. Al Gore advised the assembled nations to ignore his president's lame duck intransigence. The executive secretary of the convention fled the dais in tears of frustration as he saw his work about to go down in flames. The head of the United Nations read the riot act to the delegates, warning they would not be forgiven by future generations if they failed to act on global warming. The meeting was extended for an extra day.

Then, just as the United States was about to throw in it's veto, the delegate from the tiny island nation of Papua New Guinea stepped to the microphone and turned toward the United States, "If you are not prepared to lead on global warming, then please get out of the way." The conference broke into a spontaneous and extended round of applause. After fervid consultations, the United States delegation withdrew its veto and announced it would go forward with the consensus. Hollywood couldn't have written a better script.

But what had actually happened? Behind the scenes, a group of influential American companies had become increasingly frustrated that they were being left out in the cold as their European competitors picked up hefty contracts to develop technologies to fight global warming. Many of the their competitors were the same companies I had visited in Switzerland only months before. American businessmen wanted clear cut regulations and a stable framework so they could also profit from the upcoming bonanza in green technologies. In the eleventh hour, they had finally stepped in to convince the U.S. delegation to go along with the European plan.

Of course none of this would affect Chatham's problems with sea level rise in any kind of direct way. Once carbon dioxide is released into the atmosphere it stays there for over a hundred years. Communities like Chatham, and New Orleans, will have to continue to deal with the effects of carbon dioxide released during the past century. If today's negotiations are successful they will only affect sea level rise a hundred years from now!

Meanwhile, the La Nina winds continued to blow. Every week another storm emerged from the Pacific Ocean, dipped south to pick up humid air from the Gulf of Mexico and slammed into

Cape Cod's outer beach. Every morning I would go online to see how the Harriss camp had fared. I had grown accustomed to its slightly anthropomorphic face with its door, two windows, and a cupola set at a jaunty angle. It seemed to watch with stoic curiosity as the waves lapped ever closer. The day before Christmas I took pictures every fifteen minutes as the waves rode in on an five foot tide. In three hours they tore forty feet off the low dune that was all that stood between the Harriss camp and oblivion. The camp was now less than a house length from the swift waters of the advancing inlet. I knew the entire Harriss family was also watching from monitors scattered across the country. At least 40 of us had to wait in queue to control the Inletcam. I hoped for them that the inevitable would not happen on Christmas day.

Christmas passed, but December 27th loomed ominously. The weather called for rain and twenty mile an hour winds, but the tides were still high and the day before there had been less than a house length from the Harriss camp to the inlet. I connected to my server and the latest news popped up on my screen. Benazir Bhutto had just been assassinated in Rawalapindi. This came as a deeply personal shock. I had met Benazir thirty years before while we were doing our laundry in a Harvard dorm. She was easily the most impressive person I have ever met. First, she was striking beautiful. At least half the male population of Harvard and Oxford had released a collective groan of disappointment when she had agreed to an arranged marriage in Pakistan.

Beyond that, I had never met a person who knew so precisely what she was going to do with her life. While we folded our laundry and bundled our socks, she told me how her father had been executed by a military coup and how she intended to run for president of Pakistan. After that brief encounter I had followed her career as she rapidly fulfilled what she saw as her destiny. I was mesmerized with her style, charm, and intelligence. She was the Kennedy dynasty on steroids. Her assassination seemed like a bad omen. With foreboding I once more opened the Inletcam.

Ten foot waves were breaking both in front and behind the Harriss camp. The inlet was less than twenty feet from the camp's eastern wall. At 3 p.m. waves started to hit the house and she lurched to the side tilting precariously toward the southeast.

The Harriss camp seen on the Inletcam, December 27, 2007.

Unfortunately I had to catch a plane that evening, so I shut off my computer wondering if the camp would make it through the night. The next morning was surreal. The La Nina winds were continuing to blow and thirty foot waves were slamming into the oceanographic pier of the Scripps Institute behind our Californian hotel. There were reports of surfers riding record breaking eighty foot waves on the Cortes Bank a hundred miles offshore. It felt as if the same waves were traveling over the continent and washing up on Nauset beach two thousand miles away. I turned on my laptop and focused in on the tip of the outer beach. What had once been the hundred year old Harriss camp with a lively personality, was now just an inanimate pile of rubble. It was almost too depressing to watch.

Gradually I realized that I was witnessing the end of a culture—a culture that shared more with the island nations of Bali and New Guinea than the mainland culture of the United States. When the Crowells, the Broads, the Harrisses, and the Eldredges were in their camps they lived without electricity or running water and spent most of their time gathering food as their ancestors had for generations before. Now a way of life was coming to an end, and I was watching it on the Internet, two thousand miles away. It was a deeply frustrating way to end the year of 2007.

A calm day on the outer beach.

Chapter Fifteen
Fred's True Love

January 12, 2008

Donald Harriss drove our camera crew back to the inlet on January 12th. It was a pleasure watching another real expert navigate the beach. We had seen a lot of inexperienced drivers on previous trips. The problem was SUV's. Twenty years ago the only vehicles you ever saw on the beach were jeeps, modified beach buggies, and a few relic woodies. But ever since car companies started to make SUV's, drivers have been bombarded with advertisements of carefree young drivers cruising casually up and down mountains and dunes. What they didn't show was what could happen to a novice on a winter beach. Beach driving is a lot like skiing. You have to be able to plan ahead, read the sand and make the kinds of judgments that only come with years of experience. Even with that, you are still only a split second from being hit by a wave or stuck in the sand for hours.

Several times Donald drove us a few hundred feet down the outer beach only to decide the sand was too deep or the berm was too narrow. Then we had to reverse the car and carefully back down the beach until we could safely cross back through the dunes to the inner road. He also explained the rule of thumb to use when you did get stuck.

The Cupola House.

"First you have to thoroughly dig out your vehicle, then you dig for another half hour just to be sure. You only have one chance to get out. If you try and fail you will only have to dig yourself out all over again because your tires will have dug an even deeper hole."

Coming off the beach, we had to pass by two broken down vehicles. This was a serious breach of beach etiquette. But Donald could see that the first vehicle had gotten stuck and the second hadn't been to get around him so it had become stuck as well. If we stopped we would only add to the problem. Donald saw the situation developing a hundred feet before we reached the cars, and was able to break out of the ruts and drive down the beach slope and back up again before a wave caught us broadsides. Donald had to roll down the window and apologetically yell in passing,

"I'm sorry, but we can't stop. We'll only get stuck as well!"

"That's alright Mr. Harriss, I understand. Sunoco station's comin' down in half an hour."

It reminded we once again how well-known and respected Mr. Harriss was to all the regulars on the beach. But Donald felt guilty for the rest of the day and was chagrined that he had been recognized!

We arrived at the end of the beach before high tide. Because of the holidays, I hadn't been able to get back to the inlet for almost a month. Everything had changed. I couldn't see any remnants of either Donald's or Russell's plots of land. Both were now permanently underwater. Two acres and two houses had disappeared without a trace in less than two month's time.

Something else had changed as well. Since April, two spits had built up on either side of the new inlet. The last few times I had been out to the beach, I had noticed how much the northern spit had slowed the tidal currents sweeping in and out of Pleasant Bay. This was no longer the case. During the past month currents had scoured the spit away. Now the old East Channel that empties Little Pleasant Bay surged through the inlet at a full eight knots. It was becoming deeper, wider and more efficient with every tide and storm.

In aerial photographs you could see that the East Channel had probably been scoured when an old inlet had been this far north in the late 1800s, more than a hundred years ago. Suddenly what was happening started to make more sense. Now there were two, virtually independent, inlet systems. The old southern inlet was supplying water to the western side of the bay, the new northern inlet was supplying water to the eastern side of the bay, and a string of shoals and islands were forming to keep the Big Pleasant Bay and Little Pleasant Bay systems separate. This helped explain why the second inlet hadn't filled in last April and why the new inlet was continuing to migrate so far north. Evidently it had done the same thing when the last time the cycle started back in 1846, as well as in the 1700s and 1600s cycles. It also meant that the two systems were not acting as a simple two inlet model would predict. A lot depends on conditions that had been created a hundred years before an inlet opens.

This was a dramatic departure from what we had come to expect. Scientists had previously devised a simple theory to explain the Nauset cycle. The beach would become longer and thinner until a break occurred opposite Minister's Point, then the process would start over again until it repeated itself in another 140 years.

This simple theory had led scientists to assume that when the 1987 inlet opened it would act as a safety valve to release hydrologic pressure on Pleasant Bay so another break would not occur further north. But now we were starting to realize that there was a lot of variation within this basic pattern.

This is usually the case. Nature is a lot more complicated than the simple theories we devise to explain it. This realization would have disturbing implications for the future. It meant that the new inlet would continue to widen independently of the old inlet, and that more new inlets could open up even further north. The entire barrier beach system had broken down under the influence of sea level rise and would remain so for several decades until it could regroup and reform. This would have severe repercussions for the future of Pleasant Bay.

The immediate impact was dramatic enough. It was simply frightening to stand at the end of the beach. Six foot waves and eight knot currents were surging through the inlet. If one of the waves caught you off guard you could be swept underwater and drowned in a single terrifying instant. Standing beside the inlet was more like standing beside an angry swollen river than on the edge of the Atlantic Ocean.

However, the most dramatic feature on the beach was Fred Truelove's camp. After the no-name storm knocked the camp off it's foundation in 1991, Fred had rebuilt it on pilings buried 26 feet deep in the sand. The camp rested on these pilings six feet above the beach so waves could wash under it during storms. Dozens of brightly colored lobster pots hung from the deck of the camp, souvenirs Fred had collected from every past storm.

Now six foot waves were tearing at the sand dune beneath Fred's camp and each wave swept away another foot of sand. A loud crack and the sound of splintering wood announced that yet another piece of superstructure was being wrenched off the house. We watched as two staircases and a shower stall were systematically torn away. Fred's well built outhouse tumbled over and became lodged beneath the camp where it sloshed back and forth against the pilings before it broke free and washed through the inlet.

Each wave was undermining the Truelove camp.

Just before the last set of stairs broke off several people went up on the camp's deck to take pictures. I went out to the edge of the eroding sand dune to get a picture of their foolhardiness. Every wave would shear another two feet of sand off the edge of the sand dune and it would collapse in the roiling waters six feet below me. As the last person scrambled off I shouted,

"I'm not sure who is dumber, you taking pictures of me from the deck or me taking pictures from this sand dune!" It was Kevin Eldredge who laughed heartily. He was spending the winter in Backlash, his family's camp only two camps down from the rapidly expanding inlet.

After all the people came off the deck without incident, I, of course, had to go out there and try it myself. It was clear it was then or never. The last set of stairs was shaking with every blow. However, as soon as I climbed up onto the deck, all the shuddering ceased. I realized that the pilings and the camp itself were still solid as a rock.

In less than two hours we had watched 20 feet of sand wash away from beneath Fred's camp. When the tide finally turned, the camp remained dangling on its stilts twelve feet over the beach. The most unnerving part of the entire incident was that it had all happened on a warm, calm sunny day with little wind, and only moderately high waves. It is easy to understand erosion during a viscous storm when ocean waves are tearing at the beach. But it is far more unsettling to see a house being undermined on a day like that. It really causes you to start thinking about the implications of sea level rise. Two more acres of land were being swept away every month, and with it another home. Chatham had become the best place in the world to see rapid sea level rise.

The following day we returned at low tide. There was Fred's camp still sitting on its stilts twelve feet over the beach. It was clear that the pilings had worked. The waves had raced under the camp and torn away the superstructure but the camp itself had been left high, dry, and safe. If the camp had still been resting on the dunes as it had before, it would have been ripped into a thousand pieces and strewn down the beach during yesterday's high tide.

The Truelove camp at low tide. The previous high tide had swept 26 feet from beneath the camp.

The scene reminded me of the first time I had visited Dauphin Island on the Alabama coast, when I saw all these houses sitting on stilts eighty feet out in the calm waters of the Gulf of Mexico. I marveled at the ingenuity of the builders who had designed the homes so the owners could fish off their wraparound decks. Little did I realize that the houses had originally been built on the beach and over a hundred feet of beach had migrated out from underneath the houses stranding them in the Gulf of Mexico. That had happened during a full year. We were losing close to a hundred feet of sand a month.

How long could a house last on pilings during the winter in the Atlantic Ocean? We will never know. Fred had the camp demolished on January 17th. He had decided it would be less costly to remove the camp while it was still intact than to wait until it was engulfed by the rapidly migrating inlet. He had lost his homeowner's insurance after the no-name storm so he had to foot the cleanup costs by himself. But it's difficult to tear down your house when nothing is really wrong with it.

Fred Truelove's outhouse had been swept under the camp and left stranded in Pleasant Bay by the end of the day.

Chapter Sixteen
Problems and Paradigms

A Mid-January Course Correction

Something curious happened after Fred Truelove demolished his camp. Even though the tides continued to rise, the inlet slowed its expansion. You could see it on the Inletcam. Before January 17, about twenty feet of sand would be carved off the tip of the beach on every tidal cycle. But then, in mid-January, everything suddenly changed. The end of the beach stopped eroding and developed a four foot vertical face clearly visible from half a mile away. It was time to step back and investigate. What could cause erosion to increase then decrease so precipitously.

The old paradigm suggested that there is a 140 year cycle that directs inlet formation. In this scenario, Nauset Beach grows south until it constricts so much water between the beach and the mainland that a new inlet forms at Minister's Point, the point of greatest constriction.

The model became instantly popular because it had predictability, the gold standard of scientific observations that elevates a theory from being merely interesting to both provable and potentially useful. Graham Giese had used his model to predict that the inlet would open around 1986 and he was only two days off! It broke through on January 2nd, two days past the 140 year deadline! Of course Graham was willing to admit that that degree of accuracy had just been a lucky fluke. A rogue storm had just happened to hit on January 2nd. Scientists would have deemed the model to be equally successful if the break had occurred five years on either side of that median date.

But, the cycle became the Rosetta stone for understanding the Nauset Beach system because it appeared to have predicted the inlet with such uncanny accuracy. However, the apparent accuracy of the system also camouflaged its flaws. Sure, you could use it to plan ahead and to understand historical events, but it made the natural system appear to be more too deterministic, too cyclical, and too homocentric.

Although, to humans, the Nauset Beach system appears to work cyclically, in geological time, the system is actually linear. Nauset Beach is really not a six mile stretch of beach that grows and breaks every 140 years. It is actually a sixteen mile long beach that started growing after the end of the last Ice Age about 12,000 years ago. Today the remains of that ancient beach stretches all the way from Nauset Heights in Orleans to the tip of Monomoy in Chatham. In those early days, the longshore currents had a lot more sediment to work with. The glaciers had left behind piles of unconsolidated material including the South Channel Lobe, a large expanse of glacial till that used to make up the northeastern side of early Pleasant Bay. All this extra burden of sand was folded into Nauset Beach as the beach grew steadily south.

A barrier beach like Nauset, tends to grow like an amoeba extruding a bulge of sand forward from its leading edge. Today, the growing tip of Monomoy provides the perfect example of this process. On Cape Cod we like to describe the end of Monomoy as looking like the head of an Indian war club, perhaps one left behind by the mythic Wampanoag warrior Maushop as he retreated north.

People living on the Outer Banks or in Georgia would describe Monomoy as looking like a drumstick. Whatever the analogy, the result is the same, the distal end of a growing beach has a large head of beach ridges, sand dunes, and marsh covered spits and shoals. As the beach continues to grow that bulge remains behind, leaving the beach healthy and wide.

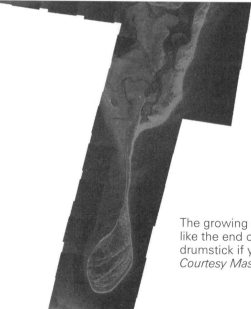

The growing end of Monomoy looks like the end of an Indian war club, or drumstick if you come from Georgia. *Courtesy Massachusetts GIS program.*

The marshes are particularly important to this process because they often double the effective width of the beach. But they become even more important as sea level rise causes the beach to roll over during storms. The overwashes dissipate their energy as they wash over the marsh, but they also bury the marsh whose peat then becomes a skeleton giving hidden strength to the overlying sand, a backbone to the developing barrier beach.

So, although we may think of Nauset Beach as stretching seven miles from Orleans to Chatham, in reality it stretches sixteen miles from Nauset Heights to the growing tip Monomoy and is almost 12,000 years old. In this more geologically centric scenario the islands and inlets that seem to form so cyclically in human time, are really just phases in a linear process driven by sea level rise.

But, if you look at aerial photographs taken before 1987, you see that there were two places that were particularly narrow and had almost no underlying skeleton of peat. These were precisely where the inlets broke through first in 1987 then again in 2007. We know from historic charts that the site opposite Minister's Point was the location of the Old Harbor Inlet in the late 1800s, and some scientists suspect that the Light House inlet formed over the site of a relic inlet that broke through before Europeans started charting these waters. Even though the inlet was filled in again during later phases of the cycle the lack of underlying peat would have left this area of the beach vulnerable.

In this aerial photograph, taken in 1979, you can see two places, one to the north opposite Minister's Point and one to the south opposite the lighthouse, where the beach was narrow and not underlain with peat. This is where the two inlets broke through in 1987 and 2007. These were probably the remains of relic inlets dating back to 1864 and the 1600s before the beach was being surveyed.

This is where it became particularly frustrating to Ted Keon that the July town meeting had not voted to fund a comprehensive study of the inlet. Ground penetrating radar could have easily shown if these two relic inlets should have been candidates for beach management before breaking through.

However, while ground penetrating radar and relic inlets could have helped explain why the inlets broke through where they did, they couldn't explain why the erosion had speeded up then decreased so rapidly. But a series of standard aerial shots could have helped.

There were other questions that still had to be answered. The most intriguing was why erosion had speeded up so quickly on the north side of the inlet. It only started becoming clear two months after Noel.

During the summer, everyone noticed the flood tide delta, the great fan of sand that had developed inside the bay. It was much more pronounced than the ebb tide delta that forms offshore and tends to be degraded by ocean tides and waves. However the ebb tide delta is particularly important, because over time it develops enough so that the longshore currents can continue to carry sediment past the inlet opening so the beach will continue growing. This happened after the southern inlet had formed. After a few years so much sand was bypassing the system that the beach south of the inlet had overlapped and welded to Monomoy making the entire southern beach a continuous growing beach once again.

What researchers wanted to know was when the same thing would happen to the north inlet. During the summer people noticed a shallow shelf forming off the north side of the inlet. This tended to slow the amount of erosion. Nobody realized it at the time because, at 25 feet a week, the rate of erosion seemed fast enough. But by December the rate of erosion had almost doubled. At first we thought it was just because of more winter storms and higher tides. But something else might have happened as well.

When the remnants of hurricane Noel cruised up the coast, it acted pretty naturally. The center of the low had passed only 20 miles offshore. But after the low passed north, its winds had shifted direction quickly to the west blowing water out of the bay. Suddenly all the water that had collected in the bay was being pushed out by the wind and rapidly falling tide. What nobody could see, however, was whether the outgoing tide had scoured a new channel through the ebb tide delta. This would have accounted for the rapid widening of the channel. Since then, each tide had flowed more efficiently in and out of the new channel and erosion had picked up from a trot to a gallop!

Backlash

Chapter Seventeen
Backlash and Batty

January 26, 2008

By mid-January the inlet had entered a new pattern. Every two weeks another storm would smash the Outer Cape and every two weeks another camp would wash away. It was like watching the New England Patriots run through the NFL . But the pattern also helped train the camp owners to become more savvy. After Fred Truelove demolished his camp, Steve Batty knew his house was next in line.

"Second Wind" had a long history. In 1970, George Costa saw an ad in the Cape Codder for a house with 200 feet of frontage on the Atlantic ocean and 220 feet on Pleasant Bay. That was enough to pique anyone's interest. George took the weekend off and drove to the Cape to see for himself. When he arrived at the real estate agent's office George introduced himself as Jim Percellis. He made a habit of never giving agents his real name. Besides he just liked the ring of his brother-in-law's name. It carried an air of substance.

George kept getting more and more excited as they drove down Nauset. When they arrived at Fran Taylor's camp, he said a quick hello then ran by the surprised owner to inspect the top of the dune. There, spread out before him was the entire Atlantic Ocean, behind him sparkled the quiet waters of

Pleasant Bay. George had never seen a place quite so beautiful.

George ran back into the camp blurting out to the astonished ladies, "My name isn't really Jim Percellis, It's George Costa and I want to buy this camp!" He bought it that afternoon, cash on the line — a steal for $16,000!

George soon learned that the nicest thing about his new camp was that it was so close to the Harrisses. John Harriss taught George how to fish and they became fast friends. As a boy, Donald Harriss remembered helping his father and George load their boat with fishing equipment, then standing around hoping for an invitation. It never came. Who wanted a teenager around to spoil the old men's fun!

The Costa camp was destroyed by the Blizzard of 1978 when waves surged through the dunes and filled the camp with so much sand it had to be condemned. George jumped through all the necessary hoops to obtain permission to burn the camp down, but he could have saved himself the trouble. It was so foggy the day of the burn that nobody would seen exactly how and why the camp went up in flames.

After the fire, George built a new camp and christened it Second Wind. This was the camp he eventually gave it to his three stepsons, Jerry, Bill, and Steve Batty.

Steve hated to lose so much family history. He had lived in Second Wind from 2002 to 2005. He had loved living on the outer beach, patrolling the clam flats as Chatham's deputy shellfish warden. At least three of his relatives had also spent their honeymoons in the camp. Fortunately it had all been before the days of the Inletcam; clothes were an optional accessory in the Batty compound.

January 21st found Steve in California using his phone, the Internet, and the Inletcam to convince his far-flung family to clean out the camp before it went under. He figured he had about three more weeks to go before the camp was washed away. But after Fred Truelove's demolished his camp a friend e-mailed Steve to warn him that waves had exposed the charred old timbers of his father's original camp burned after the 1978 Blizzard. Steve had never really understood how the beach rolled over, now he had the evidence in his own backyard.

Steve's two brothers and grown, often quibbling daughters, shared a single beach vehicle between them. But by this time an informal group of past and present camp owners had sprung up to lend support. Russell Broad let everyone stay in his mother's house in Orleans and offered the use of his four wheel drive truck. Steve figured he would still have time to fly out to the Cape in February to retrieve his small skiff and sailboat.

But on January 25th I received an emergency e-mail from Bill Ryan, the professional weatherman who had become our personal expert. Dr. Ryan told us that the three main weather models were in agreement, another low pressure area was going to bomb just east of Chatham. I forwarded the e-mail to Steve and urged him to consider January 26th the last day his family could remove valuables from the camp.

On Monday morning, visitors having breakfast at the Chatham Bars Inn thought they were having hallucinations. A house was sitting in the marsh on Light House Island. During Sunday night, twenty-five foot waves and fifty mile an hour winds had lifted Steve Batty's camp up off it's foundation and floated it a mile and a half south to it's final resting spot. There it sat serene and intact on the edge of the snow covered island.

The Batty camp as seen on the day after the Batty Storm. The camp had been swept a mile and a half down the bay in twenty-foot waves. Not a cup had been knocked off her shelves. The following morning visitors at the Chatham Bars Inn could see it grounded on Lighthouse Island. Ron Scloerb photo, *Cape Cod Times.*

When the harbor master saw the upright house he thanked his lucky stars that the camp hadn't smashed into the fleet of moored fishing boats during the all night odyssey. It had been another sad day on the outer beach, but thanks to Bill Ryan, the Battys had been able to remove all their belongings from the camp before it had been swept away.

Sunday night had been considerably different for Kevin Eldredge. He had spent Saturday afternoon standing on the Batty's deck videotaping their shed being torn off and washed away. But he thought he had seen the worst of the storm, then suddenly at dusk the wind started to howl and the snow was coming in sideways.

He had intended to drive off the beach, but now he realized that the sand was so soft and the snow so deep that he might break down and would have to wade through icy washovers and a foot of snow to get off the beach. It made more sense to ride out the storm in Backlash, his family camp a hundred feet north of the Battys camp.

He settled down in his bunk with a good book but it was impossible to read. The camp shuddered with the impact of each wave. They were breaking only sixty feet away on the other side of the low dune. The shrieking of the wind made it just as hard to sleep. Fifty mile an hour gusts were tearing at the flag he had raised to warn others he was safe in his camp. But he hadn't been able to get it down for the night because ice had frozen his pulley system.

At about 2 a.m. Eldredge went outside to check on conditions and saw no evidence that surf had breached the dunes so he returned to his fitful slumber. But the thud of a particularly strong wave woke him again at 4 a.m. This time his worst fears were confirmed. The tide had continued to rise and now waves were now surging over the top of the dune surrounding his camp with water. He raced outside to move his Bronco to higher ground. It was his only means of escape and it was standing in over a foot of water. Thankfully the Bronco started, but as he looked over his shoulder to check on the Batty's camp he could instantly sense that something was wrong. Even in the early morning light he should be able to see at least the dark shadow of his neighbor's camp. But it wasn't there. A bolt of fear ran down Kevin's spine. The Batty's camp had washed away while he had been asleep. It could have been him trapped inside the floating house as it floundered in the storm tossed seas. Kevin decided to stay awake for the rest of the night. His book wasn't really all that thrilling, but considering the circumstances...

On Monday morning I switched on the Inletcam and couldn't believe my eyes. There wasn't a trace of the Batty camp, but a tattered flag was flying from Kevin's driftwood flagpole. I e-mailed the Battys and checked again. Kevin hovered over his Bronco then walked to check out the Batty's skiff, miraculously still attached to a post in the dunes. Was Kevin trapped and going to try to escape by boat? At that exact moment our faithful Inletcam decided to get flaky and tilted wildly skyward. I knew it would take me several minutes to slowly walk the camera back to Kevin's shiny white Bronco.

The Eldredge Camp as seen on the Inletcam the morning after the neighboring Batty camp had been swept away. I could just see Kevin Eldredge's vehicle through the blinding snow.

It seemed better to be safe than sorry. I called the Chatham police. Then I remembered Kevin had given me his cell phone number. I called but received no answer, only his prerecorded message. At least his phone was safe. The police called back to report that the Coast Guard had sent out a rescue boat but they hadn't seen a sign of either Kevin or his Bronco. Had it sped off when the camera was down, or been swept away. A few hours later Kevin called back. He was safe and sound in his mother's house but exhausted from his all night ordeal.

The remains of the Batly Camp being hauled off
the beach as seen on the Inletcam.

Chapter Eighteen
The Inletcam

January 28, 2008

Two days after the Batty camp washed away I made arrangements to film the aftermath. I had to line up boats, planes, beach buggies, and finicky videographers. We had to rush, there was only a narrow window of opportunity when the tides, weather, and light would line up so we could get aerial shots at low tide with the sun directly overhead.

On the way to the Cape I received a call from the Chatham airport. The runways were still covered with a foot of snow and they didn't expect to be plowed out until noon. Suddenly nothing made sense. If everything didn't work out precisely as planned, the Center for Digital Arts would be paying three expensive videographers to sit around and twiddle our thumbs.

I called Caluh to cancel the shoot, but figured I would still continue on to the Cape to take some still shots. But after a few more miles it struck me. I could get better information sitting at home in Ipswich, than I could on the beach in Chatham. It was one of those eureka moments when you realize how much the world has changed.

When the first inlet opened in 1987, there was no Inletcam, Internet, or blogs and websites, to say nothing of SUV's to ferry you down the beach. Instead a few government sponsored experts had been given hefty grants to produce reports that hadn't emerged until well after the inlet had entered a new phase. But what people had really wanted to know in those years was what they should do in the next day, or the next week, not what they should be prepared to do in fifty or a hundred years.

This time was different. Everyone knew that the Inlet was going to stop expanding sometime, but nobody knew when and where. Camp owners needed immediate information so they could decide when to tear down their homes. If you had insurance you had to wait until a storm tore down your home to get reimbursed. But if you had lost your insurance after a recent storm as Fred Truelove had in 1991, it would be cheaper to demolish your house before a storm smashed it into a thousand pieces that would have to be removed individually from the beach.

If you demolished your camp too quickly, however, it might just turn out that you could have remained for another season, another year, or another decade. Who knew, you might even be lucky and end up like Seamore Nickerson who built his camp on the end of Nauset Beach in 1896. The beach had grown so much during the intervening years that his descendants had been able to inherit several hundred acres of land and six miles of new beach. Of course this was after the lawyers had all taken their fair share and competing deeds had been worked out!

By mid-January an informal group of amateurs and experts had started to fill in the vacuum left when Chatham's July town meeting had voted down funding for a proper inlet study. Now, local newspapers were sending out photographers to take aerial shots, camp owners were driving down the beach to take photos, and the Inletcam was providing streaming video that was so precise you could measure the rate of erosion down to the nearest foot. You could actually see a wave break against a dune then watch how the profile changed after the wave receded. People had started to realize that by pooling all these disparate pieces of information, you could actually predict the short term behavior of the inlet almost as accurately weathermen can forecast the weather.

I had already seen how Dr. Ryan's private weather reports had allowed the Batty's to clean out their camp the day before it had washed away. Now people like Ted Keon could give camp owners an accurate time frame for when their camp would most likely be hit with fatal erosion. This was practical information with real economic consequences.

Several observers had noticed that a system of rogue events and stable patterns had emerged. During a rogue event like a storm, sand would form a wide protective platform off the outer beach and inside the inlet. It would take a week or two for waves and currents to reshape this sand, then erosion would rapidly reappear. This caused the channel in the inlet's mouth to writhe back and forth slowly like a snake, or a garden hose squirting water all over your backyard.

The "Batty Camp Storm" had deposited so much sand in the system that it had caused the channel to writhe south. This gave camp owners some time. Now they could wait until the erosion started to accelerate and still know they had about a week before their camp would wash away.

However, if the channel stayed south, it might mean that the inlet had stopped expanding, and the camps could last for another season. But aerial shots had revealed a new concern. The new channel was starting to scour the delta of sand that stood between the ocean and the mainland. For the first time in a hundred and forty years ocean going waves were starting to wash up on Minister's Point.

Pam Kindler had already seen the changes. She lived on the south side of Minister's Point and she and her husband had watched higher tides and stronger currents remove sand off the barrier beach in front of their home. They and a group of neighbors had applied for permission to put up sand fencing on the beach to protect their marsh. The Conservation Commission had turned the group down because nobody's house was in immediate danger, but it had also suggested that the homeowners could renourish the beach.

The Conservation Commission had given the homeowners until April 1st to finish the job, but the state still had to decide if an environmental impact study would be required. It had determined that the beach had the potential to be a nesting site for piping plover, although nobody could ever remember seeing one of the endangered species nesting there. However, this was the first evidence that the inlet's new channel might start to affect the mainland in an appreciable way, an opening volley in what would become a protracted war.

Chapter Nineteen
Mid-Winter Blues

February 8, 2008

Winter continued its path of destruction through February. A 900 foot tanker fully loaded with liquified natural gas broke down 35 miles east of Chatham. A fishing boat with the ominous former name, "Bad Seed" grounded in Stage Harbor.

The day after the "Batty Camp Storm," the well preserved ribs of an ancient shipwreck washed up on Newcomb's Hollow Beach. Were they the remains of a three masted schooner that plied these waters before the Civil War or a shipworn coal barge that sank in the 1800s? Further up the beach, the same storm washed a nine foot rudder out of the sand and back into the sea. Both wrecks were reminders of the 3,500 ships that had foundered on these bars before the Cape Cod Canal was built in 1914.

One expert even claimed to be able to see where a left handed boat builder swung his adze from the port side of the Wellfleet ship while his right-handed compatriots swung theirs from the starboard. Grooves between the ship's inner and outer hulls showed where rock salt had been poured in a vain attempt to preserve the wood.

Of course, shortly after the wreck was discovered, the press flocked down from Boston and New York. Unlike Chatham's houses washing into the sea beside the new inlet, here was something you could broadcast from the warmth of your mobile television van. The story of a mysterious wreck ricocheted up and down the East Coast. Chatham's losses were ignored. They were too difficult to videotape.

Curiosity and curio seekers came next. Hundreds of people flocked to Newcomb's Hollow to snap cell phone pictures and enjoy the balmy post-storm weather. Jack Burrio picked up an eighteen inch piece of timber and handed it to his grandmother. A park ranger dutifully recovered the purloined artifact at the parking lot. The four year old perpetrator burst into tears. The hardened criminal already knew how to beat a federal rap, and a fine of $10,000!

Chatham camp owners were not so fortunate. They faced having to pay up to $15,000 to destroy their homes. Each owner had displayed his own distinct form of heroism. Russell Broad had waged hand to hand combat against the tide, Donald Harriss had accepted his loss with resigned dignity and gratitude that his family had been given eighty wonderful years on the outer beach. He had been rewarded by having his camp expire during the night, almost like having a loved one die in his sleep. Fred Truelove had not been so lucky. He had to stand by and watch as a wrecker stabbed a great hole in his camp's heart. It had been more like having to pull the plug on a loved one's ventilator. Eight camps had already succumbed to the encroaching ocean, but perhaps the Eldredge camp was the most difficult loss of all.

I had always wanted to visit Backlash. Part of it was the name. Who could resist a camp named for the unfortunate habit of a conventional surf casting reel to run free and snarl. This always happened just when the bluefish started to run, and you knew that everyone else on the beach would be hauling in fish as you spent half an hour picking apart the impossible tangle of fishing line. Once experienced such a cursed event is never to be forgotten.

But Backlash was also the heart and soul of First Village. In fact most old timers simply called First Village, "Backlash Village" to honor the memory of Leo Vernon Eldredge. The elder Eldredge had been a force of nature. He started Acme Laundry which became a venerable institution serving the needs of both local townspeople and Chatham's many fine hotels and inns.

"L.V." loved to hunt and fish and could build almost anything with his hands. In 1936 he skidded a shanty over ice to use as a bathhouse for his family's Goose Pond summer camp. But when the Navy took over Monomoy Island for the war effort, "L.V." lost his favorite goose hunting spot so he decided to relocate the shanty to the outer beach flyway. This time he had to dismantle the shack, load the pieces into a pair of skiffs, and ferry them over to Nauset to build his camp. He outfitted Backlash with a hand pump and root cellar and chinked its walls with salt marsh hay. A decade after building the camp he added a living room with a fireplace and built in bunks. The addition was a surprise for his son Donald and his new bride who spent their honeymoon in the remodeled camp.

Throughout the years, Backlash was the scene of many striped bass, steamer, and sizzling goose dinners. Village lore had it that one summer "L.V." found a driftwood log that was too big for his saw's diameter, so he simply lugged the whole log into the camp and placed one end in the fireplace and let the other end trail out the door. He burned it that way all through the fall and by the beginning of winter could finally shut his door.

The 1978 Blizzard broke Backlash in two, but the Eldredges rebuilt it so well it survived the 1991 "No-name storm." But, like most of the outer beach owners, the Eldredges used their insurance to rebuild rather than demolish their camps, so they had forfeited their ability to purchase future house insurance.

There was another tradition in the camps. When a family member was down on his luck, in transition, or simply needed some time to live alone on the beach, he could use the family camp for temporary housing. Henry Beston had written one of the finest pieces of American literature when he spent a year alone in "The Outermost House," which was, itself, washed away in the 1978 Blizzard.

Kevin Eldredge had followed in that tradition throughout the fall of 2007. His marriage was on the rocks and he had needed a place to live. His parents had said he could stay at Backlash while he figured out his life.

You couldn't help but like Kevin. I had first met him when waves were pounding on the Truelove camp. He had been standing on Fred's precarious deck, while I took pictures from the equally precarious sand dunes. After we acknowledged our mutual stupidity, we introduced ourselves. He was the notorious younger Eldredge, who had become something of a local hero for living in Backlash throughout all the past winter storms. For the past few months I had watched him on the Inletcam, arriving in his snow white Bronco, raising the tattered American flag that signaled he was still safe and sound and in residence. I had even envied him a little, and wondered what it would be like to ride out a winter storm. Perhaps this was our chance.

Kevin invited us in to Backlash to look around. It was a trim little camp with a huge ship's knee propped on the sand in front of the main door. Bunks lined the walls and windows looked out on the ocean only a scant sixty feet away. The "weasel room" lay off the living room. It was, of course, named for a wild weasel who had taken up residence in the camp all one summer. And there on the mantelpiece overlooking his camp, was a portrait of Leo Vernon himself.

I had to ask. Could we possibly stay for the night? I still kick myself for turning down Kevin's kind reply. It was probably the last chance I would ever have to spend a night on the winter beach.

Throughout the next few weeks I grew to know the Eldredges as they wrestled with what to do with their camp. It was a contentious issue. Seven family members held primary deeds to the camp. Some felt that "L.V." would have wanted them to burn the camp down. Others wanted to take a more cautious approach.

By this time I had started to realize how accurately we had become at predicting the inlet's behavior. At first I had thought it was just blind luck that we always seemed to arrive to film at exactly the peak of erosion, but after it happened several times I realized you really could predict when the inlet would engulf the next house.

Though I ran the risk of sacrificing my status as disinterested observer, which really wasn't that much of a risk anyway, I e-mailed all the Eldredges to tell them that we could probably give them a window of time when the camp would most likely wash away. I urged them to use this information not to make too hasty a decision. Perhaps I had sacrificed my observer status, but it seemed like we had information that they could use.

But everything came to naught. After unsuccessfully trying to obtain permission to burn the camp down, the deed holders finally decided to have it demolished. It was a somber occasion on February 8. The family arrived at low tide and made a makeshift memorial to "L.V." They decorated the driftwood flagpole with flowers and hung his portrait from the pole. It was the same portrait I had seen hanging over the fireplace where he burned that summer-long log. It just felt right that "L.V." would go down with his camp. The family wept as Kevin's uncle used a back hoe to strike the first blow.

On February 14th, Steve Daniels floated a barge out to where the Batty camp still stood intact on Lighthouse Island. Piece by piece his crew dismantled the sturdy camp as Vernon Eldredge had done with Backlash so many years before. Only this time a forlorn little outboard hauled the barge back to Chatham on the incoming tide. The pieces would be recycled and chipped at the Orleans town dump. Another chapter had come to an end.

The Eldredge camp is demolished. Kevin Eldredge.

Chapter Twenty
Diastole; The Heart at Rest

March 11, 2008

After the Eldredges demolished Backlash I decided to review our record of informally predicting the inlet's behavior. The Harriss camp had taken us totally by surprise. I had driven down the beach with Donald Harriss the day before Noel and we had both agreed that Russell Broad would probably lose his house to the late November hurricane.

But what I didn't tell Donald was that when we had to move his car to avoid being bowled over by surf, I had one of those "uh oh" moments. When he asked me point blank what I thought the chances were that he would lose his house, I equivocated. I didn't want to tell a friend that I thought his house was going to wash away the next day. But most of all, I didn't want to make any rash pronouncements. I was too unsure of our data.

The Truelove camp was different. We were able to predict the exact tidal cycle when waves started to undermine his camp. Then two weeks later, thanks to Dr. Ryan's emergency weather bulletin, I was able to warn Steve Batty to empty his camp immediately because the "Batty Camp Storm" had gained strength and was going to "bomb" ten miles east of

Cape Cod. In all, we had been able to predict the precise tidal cycle when the last five camps had succumbed to erosion. But, up until the demolition of the Eldredges' camp, I had been hesitant to express my opinion to the owners.

So, the day after Backlash was removed, I decided to act more decisively. First I had to turn my attention to the next camp in line. This was a trim little cottage, with the intriguing name Diastole, which means that moment in the body's rhythm when the heart is at rest. The name instantly made sense as soon as I learned the camp was owned by a California born cardiologist. Collin Fuller was known for playing his battered up old beach guitar on evening sails in Pleasant Bay. Rumor had it that Collin had climbed Mount Everest the week after signing papers on Diastole, giving the owner fits that he would lose his sale to a mountaineering accident on the other side of the world.

But it was Diastole's other owner that really interested me. I had attended a naval training program with Copey Coppedge in the unfortunately dry, and highly unlikely naval town of West Lafayette, Indiana. I remember it as a delightful summer, when about all we had to do was play touch football, do calisthenics and get to know each other. In its infinite wisdom the Navy had put all us smart-ass Harvard students together in the same company and given us to Gunnery Sergeant Matusko, who had arrived after all the other sergeants had picked their recruits. On our first night in the program, Sergeant Matusko made a point of telling us how much ribbing he was taking from all his marine corps buddies for ending up with such a bunch of pansies.

Of course we instantly fell in love with Sergeant Matusko and bonded with each other, as social outcasts and misfits are wont to do. Our company proceeded to come in first in athletics, second in marching, and a distant and dismal last in academics. This was because we had spent most of our time writing thinly veiled protest songs and unprintable marching ditties. I still remember Copey's calling cadence with,

"Du-ah, du-ah, du-ah ditty.
West Lafayette is really, great."

He might have remembered my impromptu lectures about physical oceanography and the inherent dangers of serving on submarines. The lectures seemed to work, none of our company ever signed up for underwater duty.

I mention these sea stories not merely out of sheer self indulgence, but to also show that we shared enough experiences so I could feel free to give Copey friendly advice and he could feel equally free to reject or use it, as it suited his purposes. My advice would not have the imprimatur of a government agency or similar voice of authority.

Meanwhile our informal group of town officials, coastal geologists, and professional weathermen continued to coalesce. We were now all in touch by daily e-mails.

I was able to reach Copey on vacation in Florida and explain that we were performing an informal experiment. I was going to take readings on the Inletcam and use them to give him daily forecasts of what to expect. At the outset I gave him a four to eight day window when the erosion was most likely to reach his home. This was based on the fact that the erosion was proceeding at the rate of about 15 feet a day. If it continued at that pace he would have eight days, if it doubled he would have four days.

Bill Ryan was able to inform our team that another winter storm was due to arrive at the beginning of that window on February 26th. As each day progressed I was able to narrow the window down further. Two days before the storm hit I was able to tell Copey that it didn't look good and that, even if Diastole did survive the storm, it would only be a matter of a few days before his camp would be undermined by waves.

In the interim, Copey had been in touch with Bill Hammatt who owned the northernmost camp in First Village. Almost everyone agreed that his was the most likely camp to survive the winter. It sat on a large plot of private land formerly owned by the Viking sailing camp. Bill didn't want to end up being the last lonely camp on the beach. Hammatt suggested that instead of destroying Diastole, Copey consider moving it onto his property. For the first time all winter the camp owners had something positive they could do, instead of sitting back and passively watching the ocean tear down their homes.

But this put Copey in a race between the ocean, the weather, and the bureaucracy. In the old days all Copey would have had to do was hire a contractor to put his camp on a flatbed truck and haul it down the beach. But now it looked like Coppedge would have to obtain permission from the town, the state, and the federal government. So far the town of Chatham had bent over backwards for the camp owners. When the Eldredges applied for permission to burn Backlash they received quick approval from Chatham and the Cape Cod National Seashore, but the state had been made so many requests for further information that the Eldredges finally had to withdraw their request and have their camp demolished.

The first call Copey made was to Bill Riley. Riley was a local Chatham lawyer who had worked with the camp owners before. After five of the camps had been knocked off their foundations during the 1991 No-name storm he had been able to engineer a solution that allowed all the damaged camps to be rebuilt on pilings. Riley recognized instantly that Copey would only have to get permission from the town because although Bill Hammatt was within the boundaries of the Cape Cod National Seashore, legally he owned his own land. On February 29, Copey met on the beach with his engineer Thadd Eldredge, Bob Hayden a house mover, and Steve Daniels who had dismantled the other camps.

They didn't have much time. Bill Ryan informed us that one storm would hit the next day and another one four days later.

But he had also spotted a change in the pattern. Earlier in the winter the lows had roared past Cape Hatteras then passed just a few miles east of Cape Cod. Now the lows were tracking to the west of Cape Cod. The tides were at a low ebb and the Inletcam was showing that erosion had slowed. It looked like the system wanted to stop. Perhaps Copey had a little wiggle room.

At nine in the morning on March 5th I received a call from Bill Riley. He had been doing double duty staying up all night to shepherd Copey's move through the legal maze of pulling permits from all the requisite town boards. Ted Keon had given my number to Riley so I could feed him information from the Inletcam. It was a generous move. Ted hadn't yet been able to access the camera on his computer, and he was still a little skeptical about its value. But he was open-minded enough to want to see if this new technology could provide accurate information within such a short and demanding time frame.

After hanging up, I switched on the camera. All I could see were two tiny headlights peering through the fog. That would have to be Vernon Eldredge's grandchild Donnie Baker. Rumor had it that Donnie had visited the winter beach every day since last Thanksgiving. I didn't want to call the cops on another Eldredge!

As the fog cleared I saw eight foot waves tearing at the southern tip of the beach. Winds were gusting up to 75 miles an hour. Copey needed to know how much time he had to remove his camp, because he had run into yet another problem. Bob Hayden's wife had just been fired from her job and he was at loose ends. But he had agreed to do the job with Steve Daniels. Bob would supply the equipment and Steve would supply the physical labor and draw on his store of knowledge about working on the outer beach.

Meanwhile conditions on the beach were deteriorating rapidly. Minute by minute, gossamer blankets of thick pea soup Chatham fog were obliterating my view. All I could see was the faint outline of Copey's camp against a dense field of featureless gray. Finally I had to stop sending my reports, and turned instead to finishing my taxes. It looked like Chatham would be socked in for the day. But, thanks to good old New England weather, two hours later the sky cleared revealing that thirty more feet of sand had been striped off the tip of the beach. If the erosion continued at this rate Copey would only have three days left, and another storm was predicted for the weekend.

That night Bill Riley testified before the Conservation Commission until 10:30pm than drove Bob Hayden back to his house in Cotuit an hour away. The next morning at 7:30 Riley was back at the Nauset Beach parking lot along with Bob Hayden, Steve Daniels and several tons of bright shiny new yellow moving equipment. But there was another snag, the town of Orleans was dragging its feet about giving permission to drive the heavy trucks down the beach, and one of the neighboring cottage owners wanted indemnification because the trucks had to drive across his property as beach vehicles had done since as long as anyone could remember.

Meanwhile, Steve Daniels had decided not to move Diastole to higher ground before the storm, but to wait out the storm and do all the work the following work week.

I was on the beach Monday morning at low tide. Nobody was around. It looked like the movers were going to miss both the low tide and potentially the last day of their narrow window of opportunity to complete the work. I made a few desultory calls and decided to drive back to Ipswich. Just as we were getting in the car, Steve Daniels arrived. It was like seeing the cavalry arrive on their two big front end loaders. Four hours later they had removed the front deck. On Tuesday, March 11th, Steve Daniels and his assistant returned. They started a fascinating ballet of heavy machinery. Each drove a front end loader to the ends of the camp and held it in place so Steve could use a chain saw to cut away the underlying pilings. Then they carefully lowered it onto an H-shaped structure of four steel beams. Once they camp was in place they used the front end loaders to lift the camp and maneuver it down the beach, one front end loader driving forward and the other in reverse. By one o'clock Diastole was again at rest beside Bill Hammatt's camp, just as high tide waves were starting to lick at his old foundation. It had been an absolute last minute success.

The Coppedge camp, "Diastole."

Steve Daniels uses two front-end loaders captained by operators talking to each other on cell phones to waltz the Coppedge camp a tenth of a mile up the beach.

Chapter Twenty-One
The Wooden Tent

March 19, 2008

It is March 19, the last official day of winter. Forty mile an hour gusts blast in from the Southeast. Tomorrow, on the first official day of spring, 50 mile an hour gusts are expected to blast in from the Northwest. The wind is rattling my windows and wrenching a low moan out of our windblown chimney cover. The storm is strengthening over the Gulf of Maine, next week's storm is expected to pass to the east of Cape Cod.

I am shocked when I switch on the Inletcam. I can just barely make out the outline of an excavator toiling in the light rain and mist. The driver is hunched over in the cab, fitfully demolishing the remains of Jef Fitzgerald's camp. The low-lying camp, aptly called the wooden tent, had already been buried beneath three feet of sand during the remnants of Hurricane Noel.

But something else catches my eye. Jef's camp is still 120 feet from the tip of the beach. This shouldn't be. The last camps had all succumbed to the widening inlet. But for the last ten days the inlet expansion has slowed to only a few feet a day, despite the high tides and continual storminess. The same thing happened after the "Batty Camp Storm," in January. This hesitation seems to be a signal that the inlet

Caluh videographing the Wooden Tent.

wants to slow down. Aerial photographs show that the north channel leading out of the inlet has straightened out and no longer wants to push right up against the north side of the inlet endangering the nearby camps. A long thin shallow sandbar now protects the tip of the beach from the once encroaching inlet. In geological parlance, the inlet is coming into equilibrium with the volume of water that needs to wash in and out of its adjacent estuary. In everyday terms, the inlet is getting better at flushing out Pleasant Bay.

The remaining camps are still in danger from severe erosion that continues to attack them from the east. This has also caught me by surprise because the Inletcam only allows me to measure erosion from north to south along the end of the outer beach. I can't see erosion happening from east to west. However I do have my team of resident beach rats; Kevin Eldredge, Donnie Baker, and Nancy Fulcher who diligently drive down the beach every day and send me back snapshots, video clips, and hurried snatches of telephone messages. Thanks to them I can continue to send out my daily forecasts.

At this point, it does not look very good. All the remaining camps have experienced 30 feet of erosion a day for the past week, and are in a new and precarious race against time. Piping plovers are due to arrive on the beach any day and when they do, the Commonwealth of Massachusetts will close down the beach to heavy traffic. Contractors will no longer be able to drive their heavy equipment down the beach to move the remaining camps. The state's office of environmental affairs has determined this window of opportunity will slam shut on April fools day.

This is just the latest in a series of surprises. When the inlet first opened I paid little attention, figuring it would probably just fill back in. But a week later, when it was still open, I started to take notice. Then, when I actually started to write this book, I thought that most of the action would take place on the mainland and assumed that I would simply be an impartial observer writing about different groups of people making decisions, and perhaps suing the pants off each other. Instead, all of the action had taken place on the outer beach, and all that people had really been able to do was stand back and watch nature run her course. Only as this first winter was winding down, had people started to realize they could actually could do something to save their homes.

But perhaps my biggest surprise came when I found myself jumping from being an impartial observer to an active participant. I like to think this is natural part of human nature. Humans are complicated creatures, but one of our more endearing characteristics is that when we see a fellow species member in trouble we tend to step in to help. The transition had helped remove me from an ambiguous position. During the early days of the inlet, I felt badly for each camp owner but was also awestruck by the display of the power of nature. Although I hated to see someone lose their home, part of me simply wanted to see what would happen next. Some camp owners told me even they harbored similar mixed emotions.

I also had a job to do. I had to be ready to film when a camp was about to wash away. First I did this my simply eyeballing the Inletcam and guessing when the next front would pass by. After this informal system worked a few times I started to assign numbers to my observations and use them measure the distance between the next threatened camp and the tip of the eroding beach. As I started to use the camera to help camp owners decide what to do, it helped clear up this moral dilemma. Now instead of subliminally rooting for nature I was able to unconditionally root for my fellow species mates. I was helped in this process by an article in the *Cape Cod Times* that quoted me saying the only one more camp would probably wash away. That gave me incentive to want the inlet to stop expanding. Amazing how ego can drive your higher faculties!

However, this process was also embarrassing. I had just finished traveling the length of the East and Gulf coasts to write a book about why people should retreat from living on the beach. Now here I was trying to help people stay in their seaside homes for another week, season, or decade.

It was an important lesson. It is pretty easy to stand back and say that everyone should get off the coast. It is a lot more difficult, but much more interesting to actually work with people to decide precisely when and how they should remove or demolish their homes. Thankfully, I found myself to be a great believer in rear guard actions. I would have many opportunities to observe those rear guard actions in the days ahead. The Battle of the Beach was about to enter its final week.

Chapter Twenty-Two
April Fool's Day?

April 1, 2008

Shortly after Copey Coppedge finished his successful move to Bill Hammatt's lot, Thadd Eldredge walked Nauset Beach to take some new GPS measurements. Back at his office he downloaded this new data into his ongoing survey of Nauset Beach and used it draw up a plan to fit all the remaining five camps onto Bill Hammatt's 4.5 acre lot. Bill Riley presented the plan to the Conservation Commission and they were on their way. It was an ambitious plan. Workers had to move all the remaining camps and rearrange the location of Bill Hammatt's building, before the state's plover deadline, slated for April first.

On March 27, I drove down the beach with Donald Harriss to assess the situation. The weather was trying to turn the corner. For the past three months there had hardly been two consecutive days of sunshine, but on this Thursday the weather was clear and cold. The mood of the beach, however, was strikingly different. Someone had drawn an arrow through the neck of a piping plover on a huge billboard depicting their nesting habits.

The inner road behind the dunes was pockmarked with puddles and rutted with the tracks of heavy trucks. The end of the beach looked like an army had just beaten a hasty retreat.

In a sense it had. One camp rested on metal cribbing, half way through its move. Another rested on columns of wooden railroad ties, piled so excavators could dig a trench deep enough that they could assemble a metal framework beneath it so it could be mounted on wheels and be hauled down the beach. An eight foot high berm of sand had been constructed around the adjoining camps, and huge tire tracks crisscrossed the beach made ragged by all the activity.

The piping plover forms a shallow depression in the sand to shelter its sand-colored eggs. Both the male and female share incubation responsibilities.

"Someone had drawn an arrow through the neck of a Piping Plover." Piping plover have become the spotted owls of the East Coast. Some people think it would be more appropriate to protect barrier beaches so they can remain as the mainland's last barrier against sea level rise rather than for their role as habitat for nesting plover.

The scene was in marked contrast to when Steve Daniel's two-man team had used finesse and a pair of front end loaders to waltz Diastole gracefully down the beach. This time Nauset was cluttered with a fleet of heavy trucks, teams of movers, an excavator, and several small bobcat manipulators. I expected to see an apparition of a long-legged Sigourney Weaver swagger down the beach, mount one of the manipulators, and toss around some slimy alien.

Nerves were almost as ragged as the beach. John Shea had been working nonstop since before Easter. He told me in no uncertain terms that he thought my predictions were bunk, and that the Inletcam invaded his privacy. I marked it down to anxiety and sleep deprivation, and wondered how I would react under similar duress. But perhaps his comment about the Inletcam came more from the unauthorized eight foot sand berm he had just throw up around his camp than a strict constructionists's view of the so-called constitutional right of privacy. But I decided not to push the point. It seemed more prudent to simply withdraw and finish what I had come out here to accomplish.

The first thing I wanted to do was inspect the narrow tip of the beach. It was much as I had seen it on the Inletcam, still essentially the same length it had been for the past two weeks. In fact, it looked like the sandspit leading off the beach might have even thickened below the high tide line.

The most fascinating feature on the beach, however, was a huge bolus of sand that had lodged itself just inside the throat of the Inlet. High course tides and waves could still sweep over this shallow shoal to build what coastal geologists call a recurving spit. But what was truly significant about the sandspit was that it was now diverting the outgoing tide to the southwest. This process had held the inlet channel to the south for the past two months. In fact, at low tide you could still walk a hundred yards over wet sand to the pilings of Fred Truelove's old camp. This led to speculation among onlookers that if Fred hadn't demolished his camp it might still be sitting on its pilings, and accessible at low tide by foot! Undoubtedly, it would also elicit a letter from the harbor master stating that the pilings continued to be an obstacle to navigation and would have to be removed at Fred's expense!

However, my main concern, was to get accurate measurements of the northern camps. It only seemed prudent that if I were to make predictions of when the southern camps would wash away, I should do the same for their new locations as well. I had already made some rough estimates and been surprised at the results. Now it was important to get direct measurements and apply the same methodology.

John Shea and John Kelley's camps were both 45 feet from the ocean, so they were still about a day and a half of severe erosion from destruction. But the northern camps were a surprise. Both Todd Thayer and Bill Hammatt's camps were 144 feet from the high tide and Copey Coppedge's camp was now

159 feet away. This meant that Bill Hammatt had only nine days of severe erosion, 18 days of moderate erosion and 36 days of slight erosion between his camp and the ocean. In other words Bill Hammatt was a single storm or about a month of slight erosion from losing his camp!

This was not really news to camp owners. Everyone on the beach, indeed everyone on Cape Cod, knew, or should know, that they were only a single storm away from destruction. Camp owners also knew that by March the outer beach was at its thinnest and most vulnerable point. But they also knew that as spring approached less powerful waves would start to deliver sand back to the beach from the offshore sandbars. The beach in front of Hammatt's camp might grow as much as a hundred feet wider by the end of summer.

But what was shocking, was the realization that as long as the sea level kept rising as fast as it had for the past century, the window of erosion in front of the northern camps would continue to close. The camp owners had only given themselves, at most, one more year on the beach. No wonder there was a feeling of depression on the beach. Had the camp owners jumped from a fast sinking ship into a slow sinking life boat?

A few days later, all that could be seen on the Inletcam were two American flags fluttering in a brisk wind at the end of the deserted beach. The heavy equipment had slunk away quietly from the zone of retreat.

But now the camp owners were in violation of the zoning laws. But The Chatham Board of Appeals met to rectify the situation on Monday night. Bill Riley had to convince them and the board of selectmen to introduce a bylaw at the annual town meeting that would allow voters to alter the zoning regulations so that five families could now live in the five camps clustered on Bill Hammatt's lot. In doing so he admitted that the lot had lost 1.5 acres in the past six months. If the bylaw passed it would create a new North Village on this 4.5 acre lot of rapidly eroding barrier beach.

The by-law had the additional consequence of allowing Jay Cashman to continue renting Strong Island from the Chatham Conservation Foundation. Anyone who lived in New England knew that Jay Cashman was the mega-developer behind Boston's Big Dig. Bill Riley made the strong point that the island could never be sold. But it cast a surreal aura over the proceedings that had played out all on that April Fool's evening in 2008.

Chapter Twenty-Three
Expert Testimony

June 26, 2008

It is June 26th, the beginning of another summer of discontent. Twenty thousand people are homeless after a rising crest of flood waters rolled down the Mississippi bursting levees in several Midwestern states. Californians are battling hundreds of forest fires ignited by thunderstorms that held no water, but rained down deadly dry lightning.

The floods destroyed so much farmland that it has raised the price of corn and doubled the price of ethanol. The cost of gasoline is expected to rise as a result. This confluence of lousy weather, global warming and dwindling supplies of oil is leading to runaway inflation and worldwide depression.

President Bush has proposed opening the outer continental shelf to encourage drilling and suspending gas taxes to encourage driving. His administration has even been discovered secretly brokering a deal to get five major oil companies back into Iraq — as if we didn't know this war was just the latest skirmish in a century long struggle over petroleum supplies that started when European leaders carved up the Middle East into compliant little oil-bearing countries after the first World War. Thus far, the President's energy policy can best be described as that of an enterprising drug dealer, aggressively pushing oil onto an already petroleum addicted America.

Fortunately the public has been acting more responsibly than the President. People have been car pooling, taking buses to the Cape, driving less. U.S. auto companies have closed down factories that make trucks and SUV's and there is a six week waiting period to buy a new gas sipping hybrid. China has raised the regulated price of its gasoline, and that, more than anything, has kept our prices for gas hovering around four dollars a gallon. We have reduced our consumption of gasoline by 6 percent in less than two weeks. Petroleum producers are feeling the squeeze.

It is not as if we didn't have any warnings about this multifaceted crisis. Today is close to the 20th anniversary of the iconic day in 1988, when the nation's leading government climatologist testified to Congress that he was 99% percent certain that we had already entered the period of human induced global warming and sea level rise. The statement made Jim Hansen an instant celebrity. For the first time, the public became fully aware of what scientists had known for years. What happened? Nothing!

The oil companies mount led a smear campaign against anecdotal evidence and President Bush censored Hansen's papers. Congress has yet to pass a single piece of legislation to cut back greenhouse gases in any significant manner.

This was my prickly frame of mind as I entered the Chatham Community Center to hear a panel of experts talk about Pleasant Bay. The press release announcing the annual symposium promised that it would dispel all the "anecdotal evidence" about the new inlet. The term raised hackles on the back of my neck.

Wasn't it anecdotal evidence that suggested that smoking caused cancer, when the experts were assuring us there was no link between the two? Wasn't it anecdotal evidence that suggested that the major fisheries were in decline, when experts were arguing that the oceans were inexhaustible? Wasn't it anecdotal evidence that said that horseshoe crabs were disappearing, when experts were assuring us there were half a million healthy adults of this uniquely valuable biomedical species in our own Pleasant Bay? Weren't some of the speakers on tonight's panel the same experts who had assured us that the inlet would close back up, when it had opened only a year ago? It was with a healthy dose of predetermined skepticism that I began to listen.

The big question on everybody's mind was economic. Would the inlet let the four towns surrounding Pleasant Bay off the hook from having to spend twenty four million dollars to build a new sewage treatment plant?

The audience was soon disappointed. Ted Keon explained that though the inlet was now 3500 feet wide, the actual throat of the inlet was still only 2100 feet, effectively the same width it had been last summer. Graham Giese cautioned that while the new dual inlet system was now more efficient, it was part of a 150 year cycle and would result in only a temporary improvement. In fact the director of Chatham's health and environment department reported that water monitors hadn't even detected any water quality improvement since the inlet opened.

This seemed to be disputed by John Ramsey's data. John was a coastal engineer who had been given a grant by the Army Corps of Engineers and the Town of Chatham to model the flow of water through the new inlet system. He had taken aerial measurements of the depth and width of the two inlets, measured current flows, and produced a model that predicted that eventually there would be 1,400 acres of new eelgrass in Pleasant Bay. This came as a shock to the motor boat owners in the audience. They were used to cussing eelgrass when it clogged their outboards.

To scientists, though, eelgrass is an indicator species, that can be used to calculate water quality. Eelgrass is actually a land plant that re-evolved to live back in salt water. Because of this strange quirk of evolution, eelgrass still produces pollen, seeds and tiny yellow flowers that bloom underwater in the spring. But unlike algae, eelgrass needs good clean, clear saltwater to thrive and produce these wonders. However, eelgrass will die back if septic tanks leach nitrogen into the ground water allowing it to seep slowly into estuarine waters, like those of Pleasant Bay. There, the excess nitrogen over-fertilizes the bay, causing phytoplanton to bloom into immense clouds of sunlight blocking alga. This robs eelgrass of the ability to photosynthesis and it dies back.

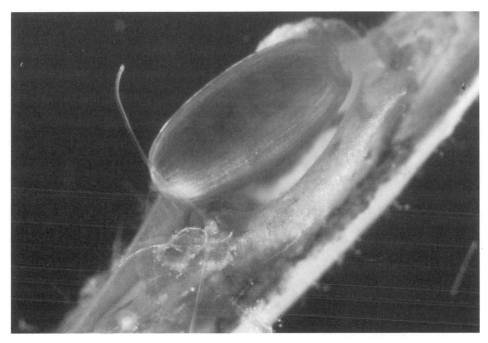

The seed of an eelgrass plant. Eelgrass is a land plant that re-evolved to live back in salt water. This quirk of evolution is what makes eelgrass such a good indicator species for water quality.

Ethan Daniels photographing red beard sponges. The inlet
has dramatically improved water clarity.

Ramsey cautioned that his model only represented a
snapshot in time, but that he had notified the Massachusetts
Department of Environmental Protection about his figures.
They would eventually decide whether the towns had to
continue sewering. It was highly unlikely. It would take decades
to complete sewering the towns, by that time the inlet would
be far less efficient at flushing our nitrogenous wastes out of
the bay.

That evening, the panelists convened at a local bar to compare notes. After an hour of discussing the Red Sox, flirting with the waitress, and consuming several large Sam Adams lagers, the experts were ready to really talk.

"What did you think about that question about sea level rise?"

"Oh, that one really had us looking at our shoes! Fortunately Graham stepped in and took it."

"Yup, he's been pushing that Georges Bank idea for years."

"What is it exactly?"

"Well, he thinks that as the sea levels rise it will allow water to flow across Georges Bank more easily, so we will see more erosion down here on the southern end of the Cape."

"But he's talking hundreds of years, isn't he?"

"Yes, but what really interests me, is that the sea level was three inches higher when the inlet opened in 2007, than it was when it opened in 1987."

"How do you figure that?"

"Well, if the sea level is rising about a foot every hundred years, that is six inches every fifty years, and 3 inches every twenty-five years."

"I see. And three inches is certainly significant. I've seen plenty of levees and seawalls collapse after only a three inch rise in water."

"But isn't that the problem? You engineers are still renourishing beaches and building seawalls as if nothing is going to change."

"That's not really true, but I'll tell you one thing. If the sea level really does rise as fast as the climatologists predict, we might just as well hang up our hats. We'll all be out of business!"

Town Hall camp.

Chapter Twenty-Four
Town Hall Camp;

Fourth of July Weekend

The Fourth of July found me up at dawn checking on our computer-controlled Inletcam. It revealed a stunning sight. Dr. Kelley's camp was silhouetted against a brilliant orange sunrise. In fact the entire southern tip of the low lying barrier beach looked like the silhouette of a submarine cruising quietly offshore. I typed in the good news on our daily web site:

"Town hall camp makes Fourth of July."

For the past two weeks I had watched the ocean as it inexorably ate its way toward the tough little camp. The tip of the beach had been losing as much as ten feet a day. Yesterday, waves started pummeling the side of the camp, and as I closed the camera for the night, the camp was slumping over to the right. I went bed fully expecting that the camp would collapse during the night and I would only see a pile of rubble in the morning.

It is impossible not to anthropomorphize these camps as each one faces the relentlessly approaching high tides. But Town hall was one of my favorites. It was the smallest on North Beach and had originally been an 8 by 10 foot chicken coop that had only been slightly remodeled. The camp had acquired its name from its former occupant, George Sears who drove a VW bug with the license plate "mayor" for his role as the titular leader of the village.

In March, when John Kelley moved his larger camp north to Bill Hammatt's property, he had left his Town Hall camp out building behind. The friendly veterinarian was hedging his bets. If the beach started growing he and his descendants could use the camp to claim ownership of the entire point. The last time this happened the beach grew to be six miles long and was worth several million dollars. If the camp washed away it would only be a minor loss. But instead of growing the beach continued to erode, so fast that on April 27 John had to use his truck to haul the camp back 75 feet off the dunes. He had to repeat the process again on June 15th. This left him with a hundred feet of narrow barrier beach between him and the inlet. The beach instantly picked up the obvious moniker Kelley's Point. But the point was not to last. The beach continued to recede by nearly 10 feet a day. This was not supposed to happen. All the experts had predicted that the beach would start growing again. But I was starting to believe only what I could actually see in the camera, not the models and predictions of the experts.

When I switched on the camera first thing in the morning on July 5th, a slight band of mist hung over the cool waters surging through the inlet. It was a startling phenomenon, the air was clear over the rest of the bay waters closer to the shore. I scanned up and down North Beach. Nothing. The tip of the beach was scoured clean, not a trace of the camp could be found. I peered through the mist once more. No doubt about it, just waves slopping up against an empty beach. I dashed off my morning report on our daily web site forum.

> July 5, 6:53. TOWN HALL CAMP DOWN: Despite foggy conditions it appears that Town Hall Camp was swept off the beach during last night's 5.7 foot high course tide.

Moments later I received a posting from Chatham's chief of police John Cauble.

> Bill, thanks for the update. Any sightings of where Town Hall Camp ended up? I will advise harbor master Stuart Smith to check out the inner harbor and beach patrol officer Jim Patterson to check out the outer beach.

Captain Cauble's message set off a wild scramble. If the entire camp had been swept off the beach, then pieces of it must floating in Pleasant Bay. With the fog coming in and boaters heading out, all the ingredients were in place for a calamitous Fourth of July weekend. Someone could easily tear the bottom out of their boat on the remains of the half sunken camp. I quickly scanned up and down the entire beach through the thickening fog. Finally, on the south side of the inlet, half a mile away, I spotted something I hadn't seen before. It looked like someone had pitched a tent on the outer beach. I switched over to e-mail and to ask Kelly Hebert if she had seen the structure on her early morning patrol. But the plover warden had already beaten me to it.

Kelley's camp is in the bayside water, heading North towards Orleans about 100 yards off of North Village, minus a roof and chair that have washed up on North Beach Island. I would try to describe it, but better yet I have sent some pictures.

Kelly's e-mail had answered one question. The roof of the camp was safely stranded above the high tide mark. But it was her attachment that really sent shivers up and down the back of my neck. There was a picture of the empty bulk of the camp drifting low in the water, northward up Pleasant Bay in a heavy bank of fog!

An hour later the fog lifted, and I could finally spot the camp on the Inletcam. It had broken into two pieces that were now grounded in shallow water about a quarter of a mile north of North Village.

Town Hall Camp. *Photo by Kelly Hebert.*

We had escaped any immediate disaster, but we still had one more hurdle to overcome. The late night high tide was expected to be another new moon six-footer. The camp would probably refloat during the night and be found drifting through the fog Sunday morning.

Early Sunday morning I sent out my first report.

July 6, 5:24 AM. NAVIGATION ALERT: It has been too foggy over the past hour to see the outer beach. But, the remains of Town Hall Camp may have moved during last night's high tide. Use extreme caution operating throughout the inner and outer harbor. Please report locations of any floating debris.

Finally, by midday, Jim Patterson had located the camp. It had split into three pieces which were now grounded and safe a quarter of a mile north of First Village. It had been an eventful Fourth of July Weekend.

Chapter Twenty-Five
Plover, Seals, and a Spadefoot Toad

July 17, 2008

It is July 17th. Our trip to North Beach Island was delayed because Kelly Hebert had to spend a day in the emergency room waiting for a tetanus shot for the cut she received on Chatham's all-terrain vehicle. In the fashion of all summer researchers, she had waited several days to get the infection treated. After all, it was the midsummer high season, her plovers had hatched and needed to be counted before they started to migrate south.

Even with a throbbing foot and a black eye from a bungee cord accident, Kelly cut a striking figure. Tall, blond and friendly she looked like the kind of bicycle cop you wouldn't mind getting a parking ticket from.

"Oh yes, everyone wants to have a drink with the plover monitor," she laughed at my borderline inappropriate remark.

Kelly may look casual, but she is totally dedicated to the outer beach. She had been out there all summer, in every kind of weather. She was the first person to spot and photograph the endangered Right Whale that almost blundered into the inlet last May. She snapped a stunning photograph of an immature bald eagle threatening the least tern colony in June, and she was the only person to locate John Kelley's camp floating freely up Pleasant Bay in the midst of pea soup thick Chatham fog over the Fourth of July weekend.

As we approached the beach Kelly gave us a running commentary.

"See that dimple between the dunes? That's where the old trail 8 used to cut through the beach. It makes you appreciate how much these man-made roads help channel washovers across the island. You can see where the water washed right under the Bloomer camp. They are trying to stop it with those piles of baled straw. But it doesn't look too good for them. It's a real shame."

Soon we are idling through a herd of a hundred Gray seals — many as heavy as a small horse.

"Most of them are bottling right now, that's also the way they sleep at night. Those big guys with the long, funny, horse-like heads are the mature males, just inside of them are the females. The infants and immature pups make up the center of the herd. It's a little like a primate colony that way."

"These guys have become accustomed to this boat. See how they let us go right through the herd, then swim behind us once we've passed through?"

"Of course the fishermen gripe about the eating their fish, and occasionally we do see a dead one with a shotgun wound. The seal probably got caught in the fisherman's thousand dollar net, and then, rather than take the time to untangle the seal, the fisherman simply shoot him and dropped the corpse overboard for us to find in the morning. Of course it's a federal offense worth thousands of dollars if they get caught. But the fishermen are more concerned about their nets getting destroyed."

The Gray seals have only been in the Bay since the inlet opened, but they have already insinuated themselves into the local economy. The Beach Comber idles near us. It is a naturalist-guided boat that takes over a hundred passengers out every day to see the seals.

"The seals have already taught themselves to do several tricks. They will do something spontaneously like roll over on their backs, and then when the tourists clap, the seals continue doing it for more attention. The tourists love to see 'em cavorting around in front of the fish pier."

"The Beach Comber's a good operation. He gives us rides over here when the town boat breaks down."

"How often is that?"

"Well, we're in my boat today, aren't we?"

The easy banter has brought us to the southern end of North Beach Island. This is prime shorebird feeding and breeding habitat. Almost a half a mile of beach has been scoured by multiple storms. We can see the process in action. Long high rollers from hurricane Bertha, stalled over Bermuda, are washing up the outer beach. They have already built a five foot high steep ridge of sand that runs for two miles along the length of the two mile island. As each wave washes over the ridge it leaves behind a veneer of sand about a quarter of an inch thick. Wave by wave these multiple veneers of sand build the beach and ridge. The rest of the water sloshes into a gully then flows into a deep pond behind the breaking waves. This is also prime shorebird feeding habitat.

Hurricane Bertha had built up a 5 foot ridge of sand. This hurricane marked the point in time when the tip of North Beach stopped eroding and started growing at the rate of about 10 feet a day.

The waves have created a unique weather phenomenon. As the cold water washes over the hot sand it generates a thin line of diaphanous mist that hangs just over the lip of the beach but stretches a mile both north and south. The waves are also washing silversides minnows onto the sand where they flop around before being dispatched by a large flock of seagulls already so fat they can hardly fly. In a week's time bluefish will trap a swirling school of menhaden against the beach and Kelly will snap pictures of the bleeding foot long fish beaching themselves in a vain attempt to escape the carnage. A neighbor of mine has seen a pair of Great White Sharks on Monomoy chase menhaden onto the beach, then flop around like a minnow to get back into the water.

Soon we start seeing plover chicks running in and out of the beach grass.

Beach grass.

"These chicks started hatching only a few days ago. See how long their legs are, and how well they run? They are one of the only birds that hatch with adult legs. That means they can start feeding themselves right away. See 'em picking up things out of the wrackline? Probably little amphipods this time of year. We would like to see if those red knots that flew in last night are feeding on horseshoe crab eggs. Tomorrow night is the full moon when the crabs lay their eggs. We can check on 'em in the morning."

"Now, that's one of my babies over there, and there is an adult. Uh, oh, there are three adults in there. That's not a good sign. An adult from a neighboring nest will come in to another territory and kill their chicks...There, now you can see the two adults have teamed up to chase him back to his own territory."

"O.K., we have two adults and three chicks, but we're still missing a chick. That's a baby, that's a baby, that's a baby. Nope, nope we have four chicks! That's the end of my work day!"

Of course, our day was only just beginning. Our next stop was the least tern colony. Kelly explained that the colony had held 80 eggs in the beginning of the season.

"Then on June 3rd the fox kits left their dens. Came back every night until the eleventh of July. They are far more persistent than skunks. As far as we know, they got every single egg. Nothing we can really do for the terns. You cant kill the foxes. Personally I would like to see them relocated, but that's somebody else's battle."

"Right now there are only seven foxes on the entire island, two adult pairs and three kits. That makes for a pretty narrow gene pool. I figure the problem will eventually take care of itself when their genetic fitness breaks down. I have a hard time with predators. When the peregrine falcon are here, do I root for my plovers or the equally endangered peregrines?"

"Now that pair over there tried to nest five times this summer. We had to build an exclusionary device around their nest but a long tailed weasel finally got in and ate all the chicks. It was a heart breaking sight. The pair had worked so hard for so long to raise their family."

The exclusionary device is a large cage that is constructed over the nest after the eggs are laid.

"It is a pretty stressful situation. You have to build the cage in 30 minutes or the eggs will die from exposure. So we have a team. One person drives the posts, another attaches the netting, while the third shouts out the time. The most important thing is to pull the top of the net as tight as a drum so the mother wont get caught in it if she tries to fly."

"But usually the parents run in and out of the bottom of the cage. We leave just enough room between the slats so they can fit through. It's only if they get stressed by a predator that they try to fly."

"Of course the predators quickly learn that a cage means free food. We had a great horned owl on South Beach that learned that if it landed on top of a cage and hooted and hollered and flapped its wings, one of the adults would scoot out of the bottom of the cage, and 'boom,' she would have her dinner."

"Sounds like a friend of mine who discovered that if he kicked our school vending machine in just the right spot, a bottle of coke would come trundling out the bottom."

Further up the beach we spotted another endangered species. This was an eastern spadefoot toad. It is unusual to see them in daylight. This one quickly hopped off the trail and started working its way into the sand.

This was a teachable moment. A young boy and his mother were coming the other way. Kelly waylaid the youngster.

"Do you want to see something wonderful? Here follow the shadow of my Peter Pan finger. See those two eyes just sticking out of the sand? Those are the eyes of an endangered toad. No, don't touch him. We'll leave him alone to dig down into the sand to get out of this hot sun. Weren't you lucky to see him?"

"Here, I have something for you. I found these sand dollars yesterday. You can pick one out and bring it home to help you remember seeing this wonderful toad."

The boy's mother beamed beside him.

"Thank you so much!"

"You are so welcome!"

I think we had just witnessed the birth of a budding new rare species herpetologist.

Chapter Twenty-Six
Playing "Wolf"

September, 2008

Hurricane Bertha ushered in several unexpected changes. North Beach had finally started its summer growth, for the first time since the northern inlet opened. The new conditions also caused a sand island to attach to Lighthouse Beach. The long, skinny, hundred-foot spit was an instant attraction. Now swimmers could dive directly in over their heads, sunbathers could walk to spit's tip, and Gray seals could lounge on its flanks.

On Labor Day weekend Thomas McDonald and his daughter walked to the far end of the new spit. On their way back, the ten year-old girl skipped happily down to the water's edge after every big wave, then turned to race back up the beach before the next wave could catch and "eat up her legs." It was the age-old game of Wolf that children had played in these waters since the time of the Monomoyick Indians.

But, on this August 31st day, an unexpected rogue wave knocked the young girl off her feet and dragged her screaming into the surf. Thomas jumped into the frothy waters to rescue his daughter, but the outgoing tide swept both of them offshore. Tanya O'Donnell sunning herself on the nearby beach instantly recognized the danger. The seventeen year-old, off-duty lifeguard plunged into the surf and after a few powerful strokes reached the panicking little girl. As the two girls treaded water they could see the young girl's father flailing against the outgoing currents.

A patrol boat should have been on station to pull the two girls to safety, but it had been diverted to North Beach to check on a group of tired kayakers. By the time the patrol boat reached the scene all the assistant harbor master could do was throw a life jacket to the two frightened girls and motor on to pick up the now motionless father. Eventually a second boat arrived to haul in the two girls. But it was too late for the father; at the Chatham Fish Pier, medics pronounced the 47 year-old Thomas McDonald dead on arrival.

It was a tragic ending to what had been an almost perfect summer. But the death had not been unexpected. Most of the 38 people who had to be rescued during the summer had been swimming off the spit, and all three people who had drowned since 2000 had been caught in the stronger current regime caused by the two new inlets.

Conditions had also changed to the north. Although North Beach had grown two hundred feet longer since mid-July, ocean waves were still eroding the outer beach from the east. Bill Hammatt was concerned. By the end of September, waves were tearing at the vertical face of the dunes only twenty feet from the back of his camp — plus, the National Weather Service was reporting that two regions of low pressure in the

Caribbean were expected to turn into hurricanes and travel north. The Service also expressed the guarded fear that the two systems might coalesce to become Chatham's worst nightmare, another giant, perfect storm.

Bill Hammatt already had permission to move his camp, now he had to line up a contractor to do the work. That shouldn't be too hard, all he had to do was call his neighbor John Shea. Shea had become an old hand at this sort of thing. He had moved three camps to Bill Hammatt's camp, including one of his own. Years before, he had used his excavator to tear down a sand dune to improve the middle road. The problem was that the dune was directly behind Russell Broad's camp. The stunt had not endeared him to camp owners who lived on the southern end of North Village. But John was more than happy to help his friend who had given him, and four other owners, a place to park their camps, until they could figure out a long-term solution — if there was one.

But Bill Hammatt and John Shea had very little time. The National Hurricane Center couldn't make up its mind what the two systems were going to do. One day they predicted the low off the Carolinas would become a hurricane; the next, they predicted it would be the one off Hispaniola.

By Wednesday morning, September 24, John Shea had his excavator on the beach, and his crew were preparing the site for the move. Although the seas were already starting to rise, most of the day should be clear enough to finish the move before the storm arrived during the critical 9:35 p.m. high tide. But when I closed down the Inletcam Wednesday evening, I could see that John's crew had only been able to move the camp a few feet. What I would see the next morning?

Thursday broke with stormy weather and almost no visibility. I could just see ten foot waves crashing over the tip of North Beach, and two gray smudges told me John Shea hadn't been able to move Bill Hammatt's camp beyond last night's location. Something must have gone wrong but I couldn't figure out what, before the visibility crashed and my camera connection went off-line.

At 2:00 p.m., NOAA released more bad news. Their storm tracking planes had just returned from flying the southern depression. It had turned into the eleventh hurricane of the season, and now Hurricane Kyle was expected to sweep into Chatham with 70 mile per hour winds and twenty foot waves — during the peak of the new moon high tides.

Later I learned what had happened on the outer beach. The sand had been too soft to move Hammatt's camp on rollers and it had become mired after only being moving a few feet. Shea had started to tear down the sand dune as the first storm raged, but it was to no avail. He had to leave the camp exposed to the whims of Hurricane Kyle until he could drive some metal skids down the beach to complete the move.

Fortunately Kyle swept over Georges Bank instead of Chatham and her strongest winds stayed safely offshore to the east of what remained of the hurricane's eye. The outer beach was only drenched by rain and washed by more waves. After a few days the beach was drivable once again and John Shea returned to level the rest of the sand dune and drag Hammatt's house through the gaping cut to its new location 100 feet from the receding shore. Bill Hammatt could finally breathe a sigh of relief.

But the story was not over, the final chapter had not been written. Copey Coppedge and John Shea only had a few more weeks before their camps would also be the edge of the rapidly eroding dunes. Even Bill Hammatt had only bought himself a few more months on his ever-decreasing property. Would the rising tides set off another expensive game of "Wolf" only this time with houses rather than little girl's feet? Would the camp owners hopscotch over each other until they eventually ran out of space on Bill Hammatt's lot? Would the town step in to stop the destruction of the barrier beach dunes so vital to protecting the mainland, or would the owners see the light and end the expensive charade?

Will the five remaining camps of North Village survive?

Whatever the short-term outcome, the long-term outcome was clear. Soon there would be no more camps in North Village, in decades there would be no more camps on Lighthouse Island and the era of Chatham's beach camps would be forever over.

Chapter Twenty-Seven
The Future

On Sunday April 6th Tim Wood launched www. chathamnorthbeach.com, a website devoted to the new inlet. Tim was the ideal person to start such a site. He was the editor of one of Cape Cod's last family owned newspapers and had written a book about the former inlet. The launch of the website was a significant event for the small town. Suddenly everyone had a place to download the accumulated reports, data, photos and videos that had been overloading their computers for the past year. The new website became both a convenient repository for Graham Giese's scientific papers, and a living memorial for Kevin Eldredge's evocative reminiscences of growing up on the outer beach with his colorful grandfather.

As far as I could tell, the website was also unique. Chatham was the first community to launch such a website, and the first community to use cameras to produce daily inlet erosion forecasts. Most importantly, Chatham was one of the first modern communities experience the effects of sea level rise first hand, and to learn how to adapt to them.

That was perhaps the real significance of the past year. Chatham had not suffered a deadly loss. During the same week that camp owners had successfully moved their homes, scores of people had died from flooding and tornadoes in the Mid-West. In September, Hurricane Ike had killed dozens more people on the barrier beaches of Texas and Louisiana. This had

The Continuing Story Of Chatham's North Beach

On January 2, 1987, a powerful winter storm created a new inlet in North Beach, the barrier beach that protects the eastern shore of Chatham, Massachusetts, from the open Atlantic. Erosion eventually caused the loss of nine homes. In April 2007, another break occurred a mile and a half to the north. As that new inlet has widened, it has either destroyed or forced the demolish of seven North Beach camps.

"Breakthrough, The Story of Chatham's North Beach" by Timothy J. Wood tells the story of the first break and its environmental, social and economic effect on Chatham. This website is an extension of the book, carrying the story forward to the present day through news accounts, photos and observations by the author, scientific reports and regular updates on beach conditions.

| HOME |
| BREAKTHROUGH |
| NEW INLET |
| NEWS ARCHIVE |
| PHOTOS |
| SCIENCE |
| BEACH ACCESS |
| FORUM |
| FEEDBACK |
| LINKS |
| UPLOAD |
| CONTACT |

BREAKS HAPPEN

BREAKTHROUGH
The Story Of Chatham's North Beach

BY TIMOTHY J. WOOD

Find Out Why

Enjoy the Four Seasons of Cape Cod

Ready-to-frame prints starting at $49, only at PictureTheCape.com

BobStaake

NORTH BEACH

North Beach is the local name for the section of the Nauset barrier beach that extends into the town of Chatham. An extension of Cape Cod's great Outer Beach, every 150 years or so, the sand spit undergoes a cycle of breaching, breaking up and growing south again. The January 1987 breach, opposite the Chatham Lighthouse, initiated the most recent cycle. **Learn more about the Nauset barrier beach cycle.**

In April 2007, a **new inlet** formed opposite Minister's Point. The two inlets are now fighting for domination of the Pleasant Bay-Chatham Harbor system. **Find out more about the new inlet.** Read news accounts of the evolution of the new inlet in our **news archive**.

"Breakthrough: The Story of Chatham's North Beach" details the geologic, social and political history of North Beach. The book provides a journalistic overview of Chatham's relationship to the outer beach. **Read excerpts here.**

In our **photo archive**, see scenes from the 1987 breakthrough and its aftermath as well as galleries of more recent photographs of the 2007 break. There's also dramatic **video** of erosion in action, and links to our photographers' websites and galleries.

Do you have a North Beach photo you'd like to contribute? Send it to us and we'll add it to our **readers' gallery**.

(Almost) Daily North Beach Photo

Taken from Scatteree Town Landing Nov. 18 at 1:47 p.m. by William McClellan.

Coppedge-Fuller On The Edge

North Beach News

Link to USGS maps of Chatham showing shoreline in 1893, 1917 and 1943 from University of New Hampshire Dimond Library. Thanks to C.W. Rice for finding this great link. (thumbnail of 1917 map below.)

Chatham, Orleans selectmen reach consensus on beach agreement. **Read the story here.**

ConCom: North Beach Camps Can't Relocate To Town Land. Read the story here.

New erosion update from Thadd Eldredge. **See below.**

Report on beach conditions from Cpt. John Cauble, Chatham Police. **See the forum.**

Coppedge-Fuller camp ordered off town land. Officials determined Wednesday that the conservation commission does not have the authority to allow North Beach camps to be moved onto town property. **See breaking news story here.**

Selectmen defer decision on moving camps to conservation commission. **Read the story.**

Coppedge-Fuller camp moved Wednesday. Selectmen were asked Tuesday to allow the camp to be placed on town-owned property. **Story and photos, including new shots of the camp on the beach, here.**

New map and erosion analysis from Thadd Eldredge. See below or **click here for details.**

Report on Hammatt camp move from **Cape Cod Chronicle, Oct. 9.**

Photos showing recent erosion of the outer beach. See **contributor page here.** Posted 9/23.

See ChathamNorthBeach.com for update information about the inlet.

not happened in Chatham. Though there had been a few close calls, nobody had died or been seriously injured because of the break up of the barrier beach. Only eight summer camps and a charming, but arguably anachronistic, lifestyle had been lost. The loss would reverberate through hundreds of extended family members for generations to come — people who had learned to endure, even love the lack of amenities in the camps. Who cared that you had to pump your water by hand, if you went to sleep listening to the nearby surf and were among the first people to see the great orange orb of the sun rising out of the sparkling Atlantic Ocean? Someone even calculated that Bill Hammatt's camp had become the easternmost house in the United States. It was also a shock for those on the mainland to look at the barrier beach and not see the familiar skyline of low lying shacks — in fact not to see the barrier beach at all!

Chatham had rediscovered one of the old-fashioned virtues of the camps, their ability to be moved at little expense. The camps had always remained modest; without running water, electricity, and only a wooden stove or a fireplace for heat. This meant that when the time to move came, all an owner had to do was to pick up his camp in two front-end loaders and waltz it down the beach. I came to call this the strategy of the wooden tent in honor of Jef Fitzpatrick's old camp. If any of the camp owners are allowed to rebuild they will do well to take the strategy one step further and adopt the Dutch strategy. In Holland home owners are given incentives to build their new houses on hulls, so when climate conditions change they can float their houses to a new, safer location.

But, the end of the first year of the north inlet also marked an ominous new beginning. For the next fifty years Chatham will have to contend with its rapidly deteriorating barrier beach system. The camps of the new North Beach village may wash away in as little as a year's time. They will be followed by the Lighthouse Island camps in the decades to come, and the era of the Nauset Beach camps will be over.

As the barrier beach breaks down, new inlets will allow major storms and Atlantic surf to start undercutting mainland bluffs and houses that had been safe for the last 140 years. These will not be $100,000 summer camps that can be picked up and carted away by a front-end loader, but multi-million dollar McMansions, holed up behind expensive erosion control fortifications or, more likely, pitchpoling down Chatham's imposing high cliffs.

Will this muti-million dollar McMansion be next?

Whatever the future brings, hopefully the world will have learned a few lessons from Chatham's experiences. In a single year, the small village had to deal with the effects of sea level rise that most coastal communities won't experience in fifty years. Other barrier beach systems will collapse as storms increase and sea levels rise.

As if to accentuate this point, on September 13th, 2008, Hurricane Ike devastated Galveston, Texas, and Bolivar Peninsula; twin barrier beaches, not that much larger than Nauset. If there is any worse place to build a city than New Orleans, sitting in the middle of a swamp twenty feet below sea level, it is Galveston, Texas, or Bolivar Peninsula, sitting on barrier beaches only a few scant feet above sea level!

Instead of being able to move like the camp owners of Nauset, Galvestonians and Bolivarians are stuck in a repeating cycle of destruction, where their only recourse is to evacuate in the face of increasingly frequent hurricanes, or stay and face what the National Weather Service has warned will be "certain death."

On September 8, 1900, during what became known as simply the 1900 Storm, between 6,000 and 10,000 people had been swept off the streets of Galveston into the shark filled waters of the Gulf of Mexico. After the storm, the city responded by building a three mile long, twenty-foot high seawall, to protect against future storms. Despite the wall, the city never recovered its former glory as the busiest port and wealthiest city in Texas. The same thing happened on September 13, 2008, when hurricane Ike devastated the twin barrier beach islands of Galveston and Bolivar Peninsula again — only this time the seas had risen a foot higher.

So, what will happen when the Antarctic and Greenland land glaciers melt and sea levels rise 23 feet in the coming decades? Then, it will not be the simple summer camps of Nauset, or the modest homes of Bolivar Peninsula, but the high rises of coastal cities like New York and Boston that are destroyed, and the barrier beaches of Miami and Atlantic City that wash away. Will they have learned Chatham's lessons? Will they be able to move and start over?

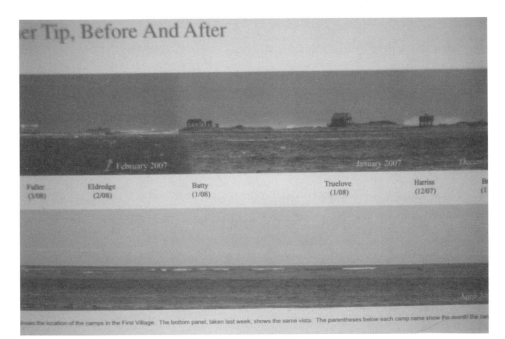

February 2007 January 2007 December

| Fuller (3/08) | Eldredge (2/08) | Batty (1/08) | Truelove (1/08) | Harriss (12/07) | Br (1 |

...ws the location of the camps in the First Village. The bottom panel, taken last week, shows the same vista. The parentheses below each camp name show the month the cam...

This photo mosaic shows North Beach as it was in 2007. By 2008 all that could be seen was open water.

Epilogue

It is December 22, 2008. Cape Cod has just been lashed by two December storms with 20 foot waves and 50 mile per hour gusts. As this book goes to press, Chatham is still waiting to hear how the remaining North Village camps fared. Owners are particularly eager to see if the Coppedge camp was spared.

On December 9, the Diastole was moved again, this time off the rapidly eroding high dunes on the east side of the beach to a lower, seemingly more vulnerable spot on the west side of the beach. All the other camps had been moved to avoid erosion; this was the first camp to move to gain the advantage of the now rapidly growing beach. If Copey Coppedge's gamble worked it meant that other former camp owners might be able to rebuild their camps as the beach grew back into their former property lines. This would mark the dawn of a new era in the way barrier beaches are managed.